Innovations in Legal Project Management

GENERAL EDITOR: AILEEN LEVENTON

Commissioning editor
Alex Davies

Editorial assistant
Francesca Ramadan

Published by
Globe Law and Business Ltd
3 Mylor Close
Horsell
Woking
Surrey GU21 4DD
United Kingdom
Tel: +44 20 3745 4770
www.globelawandbusiness.com

ISBN: 978-1-78358-352-2
A catalogue record for this book is available from the British Library

Contents

Executive summary

The organizational competence of project management provides a solid foundation for every activity conducted by a business and the practice of law. Legal project management (LPM) provides the discipline that enables lawyers and those who manage legal work – in law firms, law departments and alternate legal services providers – to define, demonstrate and deliver greater value by balancing the scope of work, time, and resources as they strive for optimal efficiency, outcomes and client satisfaction.

Although many distinguish the business of law from the practice of law, innovators in legal project management take an integrated approach. In commercial and governmental settings, practicing law is not an academic exercise, nor an end in itself. Effective legal services address a client's business needs, opportunities and risk profile, and may also implicate public policy and legal precedent. The client experience is personal as well as professional. LPM provides a framework for meeting all these challenges.

Some perceive LPM as complex; it is in fact what lawyers already do. However, it requires a more systematic approach, using the language of business. At its core, effective project management is about sound communication at critical points with the right stakeholders. These audiences range from colleagues to clients; include peers, subordinates and leadership; and vary from external law firms to regulators. LPM is a mindset as well as a discipline; it concurrently has a tight structure and a loose fit.

To explore innovation in legal project management, it is necessary to have a baseline understanding of LPM practices. In the past 10 years, client needs and expectations for the delivery of valuable legal services have created significant pricing pressure and competition among law firms and other service providers. Law departments, inside counsel, and other professional staff numbers have also grown. Demand in meeting the needs of the business ("internal clients") in a cost-effective manner has accelerated. Legal project management, process improvement techniques such as "Lean", data analytics, knowledge management, the increased stature of legal operations professionals (previously referred to as "non-lawyers"), and technology have all provided a portfolio of resources for meeting the challenge of providing cost-effective and valuable legal services. During this time, legal project management has gone from being perceived as another management fad to broad acceptance and utilization, with LPM requiring a stand-alone or well-integrated legal operations/practice management function.

A baseline of LPM practices at law firms has developed; a cadre of legal project management professionals have self-organized in the True Value Partnering Institute; and training programs that build awareness abound. Corporate law departments have adopted legal project management practices through their intake of client requests and allocation of work internally and to external counsel. All provide useful tactics.

None of them are covered here. Instead, this book profiles those who have done the difficult work of harnessing the relevant aspects of legal project management as a strategy that is explicitly aligned to a law firm's or legal department's business objectives and culture. The authors describe communication strategies and techniques to train, coach and mentor those acquiring the skills to implement legal project management practices as a core aspect of the firm's business strategy, operations, quality legal services, and focus on the client experience.

All the contributors to this book are professionals who continuously see around corners in improving the legal profession. They have created value for their firms, clients, and organizations; others have advanced the legal profession. The contributors – coming from both domestic US and global organizations, representing both practicing lawyers and other industry experts – have systematically:

- Used deep insights about particular clients to create new services and ways of doing things that impact the client's business goals;
- Incrementally improved the speed, value (cost/margin), and quality/benefits of the product or service they deliver; and/or
- Relied on technology that is home grown or highly customized to meet users' needs.

The book opens with Meredith Mendes – the executive director and chief operating officer of Jenner & Block – taking inspiration from Albert

Einstein in chapter one: when the facts don't fit the theory, change the facts. She points out in a detailed case study how this paradigm can be a useful guide when trying to find the best solution for law firm budgeting and process improvement tools. This chapter explains how an AmLaw 100 firm explored existing and emerging legal industry options and ultimately created a bespoke LPM program that reflected the firm's unique culture, values, and client demands.

In chapter two, Randall Brater and Katie Heilman – practicing lawyers at Arent Fox LLP – describe how their law firm undertook several programs with client teams to improve efficiency and realization. They extracted lessons on how to improve internal and external communication and client satisfaction, while increasing realization and better management of the firm's resources. The authors point out that although education and training on these issues and project management is important, implementing these techniques can prove difficult. Several case studies are provided as an illustration of how they achieved success. This chapter describes a client-facing initiative geared towards improved communication, efficiency, and realization; an internal team project aimed at better understanding responsibility, scope, and leadership for certain tasks and reports for clients; and a budgeting and timekeeper tracking system that includes buy-in from associates to improve time recording, workflow distribution, and management of resources.

Next in chapter three, the focus is on both customization and the substantive practice of law with Dennis White, counsel at Verrill & Dana, and Byron Kalorgerou, a partner at McDermott, Will & Emery, seasoned mergers and acquisition counsel. As the co-chairs of the American Bar Association Task Force on Legal Project Management in Merger & Acquisition Transactions, they demonstrate how LPM can be most impactful with tools and techniques tailored to fast-paced M&A transactions that are often multi-jurisdictional and always business-driven. The legal work involves multiple specialties and a variety of players. The authors describe how the Task Force has produced practical tools grouped by the phases of an M&A transaction (deal, pre-deal, and post-deal), along with several budgeting and billing tools that span the matter.

Taking customized tools to the next level, in chapter four Todd Hutchison – founder and leader of the global organization, the International Institute of Legal Project Management – discusses scalable and innovative training in legal project management. The transition from law students' historic physical presence in libraries has been replaced with online resources, and law schools have progressed from pure face-to-face education to models that include complete online delivery. This chapter explores how technology is enabling global training opportunities, and what the virtual classroom may look like in the future.

In chapter five, Thomas Agostinelli, director of practice management at a major regional law firm, moves from high-tech to show how simple meetings can be synonymous with innovation. With helpful anecdotes, he discusses a technique used in agile project management. Used extensively in many industries to maximize the daily effectiveness of a team engaged in any type of project, stand-up meetings also promote organization effectiveness. This chapter explains when, why and how to implement 15-minute stand-up meetings – a minimal investment that can maximize efficiency and profitability at any law firm or legal department of any size or culture.

Moving to the client perspective, in chapter six Kathleen Thompson, MBA, PMP, highlights the unique program developed by a national law firm when it brought her in from a midwestern Fortune 500 company. In her business role, she had influence over payment of substantial legal fees to major law firms for significant transactions. Her firsthand knowledge of what drives the satisfaction of the business people (vs inhouse counsel) highlights how leadership outside the legal department can control the law firm selection process, ensure the timely payment of invoices, and make demands for budget and status updates. The chapter provides a case study and makes recommendations for implementation of successful LPM programs.

Building on the importance of providing value to clients, in chapter seven Kevin Bielawski and Lann Wasson – director and associate director of legal project management, respectively, at Husch Blackwell – point out how legal project management is most effective when law firms and clients actively collaborate. In this case study, the authors describe the benefits of their firm's deep understanding of their client's business needs, which required alignment of teams, projects, financial reporting and measurements of success. They show how hard financial metrics, new value metrics, and their success stories demonstrate that LPM is an excellent approach to contain cost and deliver exceptional client service.

In chapter eight, Davis Wright Tremaine's (DWT) legal business solutions director, Sam Davenport, and DWT practice economics director, Brian Fanning, assert that today's LPM framework focuses heavily on the production of excellent work product but largely ignores its delivery to the client. They predict that as more law firms adopt LPM tools and clients begin to demand legal work be delivered in ways tailored to business priorities, the gap between excellent work product and highly satisfied clients will continue to grow. To address that gap, the authors review the history of DWT's award-winning innovation department – DWT De Novo – as a case study in building service delivery innovation at a law firm. They identify six cultural biases that keep most law firms from easily innovating, and describe how DWT De Novo overcame each bias. Fanning and Davenport present an approach law firms can model to expand their existing LPM framework and span the gap between excellent work product and client delight.

Continuing the focus on the client and closing in chapter nine, Aileen Leventon – principal of Edge International and the contributing editor of this book – discusses how law departments are able to effectively implement LPM tools to support their strategy to add value to the corporate bottom line. Drawing on her work for corporate clients, law firms and key legal industry trade associations, Aileen first defines the role of the legal department by its fundamental challenges: how to provide cost-effective legal services by doing the work inside; diplomatically rejecting a request from a client to do work that really does not require the attention of scarce legal resources; or retaining external counsel or other support. And once this decision is made through a formal or informal intake process, she shows how lawyers can scope, plan, conduct, monitor and review the work quality and client needs. She provides a common-sense discussion of LPM concepts that may be used by lawyers in law firms, legal departments and government agencies.

Taken together, these 13 authors show that innovation takes many forms. It is not necessarily costly, nor does it need to change the industry. It can be based on altering a mindset or developing customized tools. Each contributor to this book has demonstrated a commitment to continuous improvement in a manner that satisfies their respective stakeholders' perception of value. That commitment is truly the innovation that has an impact on both the innovator and the beneficiary of the careful execution of the innovator's strategy.

About the authors

Thomas Agostinelli serves as director of practice management at Butler Snow LLP, where he collaborates with practice group leaders to develop strategies to best serve the client and streamline business operations. His role also includes oversight of paraprofessionals, litigation support and project and process management within Butler Snow, where he drives legal project management (LPM) and process improvement initiatives to enhance delivery of legal services and client satisfaction. Prior to joining Butler Snow in 2013, Thomas worked at Horne LLP where he supported government disaster recovery programs with the Government Services Practice Group. Thomas is a certified project management professional (PMP) and an accredited legal project management professional (ALPMP).

Kevin T Bielawski is the director of legal project management and strategic pricing at Husch Blackwell, and has 21 years of experience in the legal industry in various financial roles. In his current role, he consults directly with the firm's partners and its clients to identify business objectives, value perspective, process inefficiencies, and assist with solution development and implementation. He regularly leads the development, proposal and execution of appropriate fee arrangements that meet clients' budget demands. He is an accredited legal pricing professional and a certified project management professional.

Randy Brater is a partner and commercial litigator at Arent Fox, who represents companies in the health care, life sciences, construction, food, fashion, and media and entertainment industries. He routinely litigates high-stakes matters in state and federal courts in cases involving the False Claims Act, trademark infringement, unfair competition, and other Lanham Act claims, and data compensation arbitrations arising under the Federal Insecticide, Fungicide and Rodenticide Act (FIFRA). For the past several years, he has served as the project management task force leader at Arent Fox, overseeing projects in various practice areas designed to create efficiencies with clients and foster accountability, communication, predictability, and transparency.

Sam Davenport is the director of legal business solutions at Davis Wright Tremaine, where he manages the DWT De Novo's Legal Solution Architects. He holds a JD from Rutgers School of Law, a PMP from the Project Management Institute, a CSM and CSPO from the Scrum Alliance, and an LPM certification from the LPM Institute. He is a recognized expert in project management and business operations, routinely presenting and speaking on those topics at legal industry conferences.

Brian Fanning is the director of practice economics at Davis Wright Tremaine. He holds an MBA from the Foster School of Business at the University of Washington and is an accredited legal pricing professional through the True Value Partnering Institute. Brian leads a team charged with leveraging the firm's economic and operational data to drive more effective, profitable decision making. Brian's team is also responsible for developing and articulating the firm's data strategy and developing reporting capabilities that deliver data, analysis, and insights to end users at every level within the firm.

Katie Heilman is an associate in Arent Fox's complex litigation group. Her practice focuses on ERISA and managed care litigation, environmental litigation and regulatory counseling, and fashion/retail law. She has been involved in litigation matters in state and federal court, as well as arbitrations, and is experienced in all phases of litigation, including discovery, depositions, motion practice, trial preparation, and appeals. Katie has counseled clients on regulatory compliance and litigation strategy in a wide range of industries, including fashion and luxury goods, real estate, health care, agriculture and biotechnology, media and entertainment, and hospitality.

Todd Hutchison is an international bestselling author, global consultant and educator, and an adjunct associate professor in project management. He was formally a global board director of the Project Management Institute, and the inaugural Fellow of PMI in Australia, with over 30 years' experience in leading projects. Todd leads the global management consultancy and training group called Peopleistic, including the Peopleistic Legal PM division, and also holds adjunct positions with CQUniversity, Edith Cowan University and Curtin University. He has worked in over 150 organizations across 13 countries and is the chairman of the International Institute of Legal Project Management.

Byron S Kalogerou is a partner at McDermott Will & Emery LLP. He focuses his practice on domestic and cross-border mergers and acquisitions, joint ventures and alliances. Byron spent 17 years in-house before returning to law firm life 14 years ago with a desire to bring his keen sense of the "voice of the customer" to drive predictability and efficiency into the M&A deal process. He is a pioneer in using legal project management and co-founded and co-heads the Task Force on Legal Project Management in M&A of the Business Law Section of the American Bar Association, and served as co-editor of the ABA guidebook entitled *Using Legal Project Management in Merger and Acquisition Transactions*, now in its second edition. Byron also created the first-of-its-kind web-based collaborative deal management portal, which McDermott has adopted and embraced as the M&A Gateway. He regularly speaks on the topic and on how using legal project management in M&A results in greater client satisfaction and retention.

Aileen Leventon is a business counselor to the legal industry and a practicing lawyer with over 30 years of experience. She consults with law departments, law firms and individual lawyers on strategies to manage and sustain sound financial performance and continuously improve the efficiency of legal work. In addition to advising, coaching, and training, Aileen has facilitated numerous after-action reviews of closed matters to promote buy-in of legal project management techniques. She has also been embedded in ongoing matters to provide analysis and coaching to bring distressed matters back on course.

Meredith Wise Mendes is Jenner & Block's executive director and chief operating officer. Meredith provides strategic direction, financial analysis and operations management for all Jenner & Block offices. She has a long track record of creating top-line growth and increasing net income by driving innovation and efficiencies, metrics and process improvements, and implementing management tools that further the firm lawyers' ability to provide excellence in client service. Before joining Jenner & Block, Meredith was worldwide chief financial officer of Edelman, a global public relations firm, and chief financial officer of Medline Industries. She began her career practicing law in corporate and municipal finance, and is a sought-after speaker on topics including legal project management, technology and the law, and real estate management in professional services firms.

Kathleen Thompson is the senior manager of client value and matter management at BakerHostetler. She has 20 years of experience leveraging her finance and project management real-life experiences to ensure a methodical and organized approach is applied to programs and projects. Her training approach provides information and relatable finance and operation perspectives. Kathleen consistently acts as a resource to provide specific guidance on managing clients, internal resources, defining and utilizing work plans and other opportunities to add value. Her ability to tailor a solution for a specific situation is how she has been able to increase profitability and client satisfaction. Recently, she was responsible for developing, implementing and coordinating legal project management (LPM) and wrote a manual on LPM, outlining specific methodology and tools.

Lann Wasson is the associate director of legal project management at Husch Blackwell LLP and is both a certified project management professional and Lean Six Sigma Green Belt. For the past 18 years he has worked closely with client teams and practice groups in their use of technology, legal project management and approaches to business model and product design. Over the years, Lann has also worked with in-house counsel to discuss how to adapt the firm's technology platforms to their needs, as well as suggest how legal project management could augment law department programs and strategies. In 2017 and 2018 the ACC recognized two of these client projects as Value Champions.

Dennis J White is senior counsel in the Boston office of Verrill Dana LLP, where his practice focuses on transactional matters, particularly mergers and acquisitions and on advising companies and directors regarding governance issues. Den co-founded and co-heads the Task Force on Legal Project Management in M&A of the Business Law Section of the American Bar Association, and served as co-editor of the ABA guidebook entitled *Using Legal Project Management in Merger and Acquisition Transactions*. He is also a past chairman of the Global Board of Directors of the Association for Corporate Growth (ACG), an M&A trade association with more than 14,000 deal community members in over 50 chapters around the world.

Chapter 1: Making legal project management work – a custom approach inspired by Einstein

By Meredith Wise Mendes, executive director and chief operating officer at Jenner & Block LLP

Like many law firm professionals, I've learned that finding the proverbial "aha" moment in a complex project can make all the difference in crafting the right solution. At Jenner & Block, deciding to create a custom approach to legal project management (LPM) wasn't the first choice, but it has definitely been the right choice.

Recognizing the real needs

That elusive "aha" moment occurred about eight years ago at a law firm conference when an e-billing software provider demonstrated the functionality of their software, and I realized our clients had more comparative information than any individual law firm could possibly get. As a seasoned finance professional in the world of professional services, I was used to dealing with project management, pricing and procurement. But when I moved to the legal industry, I didn't expect to see the same demands made of legal professionals. After years of collecting information through e-billing systems, in-house corporate legal departments were generating dashboards comparing, among other things, law firm billing rates, costs to perform work for tasks identified using American Bar Association (ABA)[1] task codes, and variances to budget by matter. The vendor also showed scorecards reflecting in-house counsel's overall satisfaction with the law firms performing the work.

Other than rates on file for bankruptcy matters, anti-trust laws prevent law firms from sharing rate information. Since my law firm was one of many that was required to use ABA codes on matters for certain clients, I figured our finance and information technology teams could simply mine information and create a searchable database from our own billing system to help our lawyers price their matters.

After that conference, we invited the same vendor to present their findings at an all-partner meeting with the goal of educating our partners on the data our clients collect on their law firms. Our partners were underwhelmed by the presentation. Shortly thereafter, we convened a group of partners to discuss the feasibility and utility of mining ABA codes our timekeepers were inputting into client e-billing systems. At that meeting, I learned the ABA codes were not tailored in a way that would help our partners manage matters or give them any insight into the number of hours and staffing levels required to complete a task.

For instance, the litigation category "Fact Investigation/Development" was vague as well as an activity that occurred throughout a litigation matter, so it was impossible to isolate to a particular phase of a litigation matter. Similarly, "Pleadings and Dispositive Motions" was not specific enough to help with pricing. Further, many of the lawyers were inputting their time using block time entries. In fact, to reduce the number of time entries for each timekeeper, some partners' secretaries were combining time entries for a single day. For our transactions and investigations work, our clients were instructing our lawyers to input just one or two ABA codes for all of their work regardless of the task being performed, because tasks needed for investigations and corporate transactions were not specific enough for our lawyers' activities. In light of this information, we concluded that using ABA task codes for our firm would be a fruitless exercise. And although our project management team (PMO) sorted through time and docketing entries to piece together the tasks performed during a matter, this was an extremely time-consuming and difficult endeavor, particularly for personnel not working on a matter.

Following the internal meetings with our lawyers, we met with several legal management software providers. But their software was either not available for law firms to purchase (they would only sell to in-house legal departments based on an internal policy that would presumably protect them from any conflicts of interest), or it was not designed in a way that would be useful for firms. We considered and met multiple times with the few vendors offering information about average costs of various types of matters in different jurisdictions. But again, the information was extremely limited, and was so general and high level that it was deemed unusable and not meaningful by our practitioners. We even met with a startup offering a matter budgeting tool, but the tool was clunky, did not allow us to customize tasks or associate tasks with multiple phases to create uniquely identifiable data, difficult to integrate with our financial system, and would have been time consuming and expensive to customize. After years of implementing enterprise resource planning software in corporations before taking my role as executive director, I was eager to avoid the difficulty and expense of customizing off-the-shelf systems that didn't have the desired functionality.

Many of our lawyers understood the importance of gathering meaningful information to help them compete on pricing with other law firms and to help them manage their matters. But no off-the-shelf tool existed that would meet the firm's needs. We even purchased normative data providing ranges of ABA-based costs for different types of matters captured from multiple anonymous firms in different jurisdictions, but there were no takers and the database went unused by our lawyers.

Developing the right tools by changing the facts

After this extensive and unrewarding search for the right software to meet our needs, the "aha" moment happened. We adopted Albert Einstein's paradigm – since the facts didn't fit the theory, we changed the facts. We started by taking into account Jenner & Block's unique culture, values and client demands. We embarked on the creation of a custom LPM program with options to select individual portions of the program, and we created custom tools that would resonate with our lawyers and our clients. We borrowed concepts and some tools from traditional project management, and set the following additional requirements: We would create a bespoke budgeting system which was fully integrated with our financial system, provide full transparency throughout the month and predictability. It also needed to generate automated comparisons of budget and actual results, and be integrated with SharePoint, so both clients and matter teams could review matter status in real time and from reports. We needed drill downs to timekeepers and views at the phase and task level. Culturally we knew our lawyers would want our financial personnel to run the systems for them, so we designed the tools to meet our financial planning and analysis team's specifications. Since our lawyers were already using SharePoint sites for matter management, we also determined that the tools needed to be integrated with sites already in use.

As part of the development of the matter budgeting tools, we worked with key partners across practice groups to design repeatable taxonomies with "JB codes" (Jenner & Block customized codes) at the task level, reflecting how those groups wanted to track their matters. Using repeatable codes would ensure the time to perform a task and phases of a matter could be stored and used for future matter estimation. JB codes could be rolled up to JB phases, and where appropriate ABA codes and phases existed we used those. For matters where clients required ABA codes for e-billing, JB codes would be mapped to ABA codes so e-billing systems would not be affected.

JB task codes would not be visible to our outside clients, and ABA task codes would not be visible to our internal lawyers so our lawyers would not have to choose from two sets of codes. Getting our lawyers to choose *one* task code was hard enough! Task codes could be used in multiple phases, but the combination of each phase and task code had to be unique for tracking purposes. Where timekeepers were entering JB codes on multiple related matters, we developed a relational database that would prevent the lawyers from choosing an ineligible task on a matter. Whereas tracking the same task on multiple matters for a client previously took hours to compile, we could now provide this information to our attorneys and the client in less than an hour.

We created a custom matter attributes database to store budgets using JB codes with key word search functionality. The matter attributes database allows us to store and recreate matter budgets for responses to requests for proposals (RFPs) and other client requests for matter budgets, and is essential for knowledge management. The program and tools were accessible from an LPM sample site, and we developed specific aspects to display on a dashboard, with stoplights showing real-time status and customizable thresholds for stop lights to change to yellow for caution, green for on track and red for items that were past due. We developed multiple tools for matter budgeting which could be used depending on the complexity of the need for detailed budgets and the number of matters being tracked for a single client. We also spent significant time modifying our financial system to allow our financial team to capture, store and retrieve the data. And we had to address modifying security so matter sites displaying task lists, dependencies, milestones, and timelines and matter budgets with comparison to real-time information were accessible only to internal and external matter team members. All of this work speaks to the flexibility of our team and our ability to modify our systems to the needs of our lawyers.

After approximately three years of below-the-radar work, we presented the products and services we had developed to firm partners and some key clients. Before our timekeepers got used to selecting appropriate JB codes, our LPM team spent significant time reviewing the time entries to ensure the right JB codes were selected. After some time with the JB phase and task code drop-down selections, our lawyers became familiar with the drill, and our LPM team hardly spent any time scrubbing time entries.

When clients asked if we had LPM, sometimes our LPM team stepped in and interacted directly with the procurement and project management personnel working for our clients. The reactions we received after demonstrations of our LPM tools to business people on the client side were positive. We also prepared presentations for partner and practice group meetings, so our lawyers could present to the partnership and our clients' in-house legal departments. Partner early adopters who presented at partner meetings reported that the tools and methodology were aiding them with matter management, and that our clients were enthusiastic about using LPM on their matters. By this time, questions about LPM and efficient matter management were contained in virtually every RFP. Having an LPM function was critical to maintaining some of the firm's key clients and helped the firm win business.

Our team has used LPM tools to track visas of timekeepers spending time working overseas to ensure compliance, create e-discovery dashboards displaying progress with customized detail not offered by outside software vendors for the lawyers managing the matters and client, for task lists managing multi-jurisdictional drafting of policies complying with privacy legislation, and most frequently for developing and managing matter budgets tracking fees and disbursements.

Adding the talent

Persuading our lawyers to accept help from other professionals and integrating matter budgeting into the legal work was not always easy. We started with one project management hire, and today, in light of demand for LPM, we have seven full-time analysts and legal project managers (LPMs) on the team in a dedicated project management department (the PMO). Some of our LPMs have Six Sigma and project management professional certifications, and experience managing projects outside of the legal industry. All of our LPMs are deployed on multiple matters and help with continuous monitoring, reporting and development of tools. Our LPMs have business, information technology and financial backgrounds, and a few of our analysts started at the firm as entry-level docketing assistants so they are familiar with litigation concepts.

This staff function has become extremely popular as a potential career path. We do not employ any trained lawyers (other than myself guiding the team) because we don't want our analysts practicing substantive law (we have plenty of skilled lawyers), and we don't bill our LPM services to clients. We market LPM as a value-added service. We believe not charging for this time creates a strong incentive to use LPM internally, and is a competitive differentiator with clients.

As part of their daily responsibilities, LPMs prepare matter budgets. They may also be required to sift through time entries to quantify tasks where there was previously block billing by our lawyers on a matter or matters. For those lawyers who have adopted JB codes, building a budget is vastly simplified by pulling existing codes. Our plan is to grow acceptance of the use of JB codes and to increase the number and types of matters stored in our matter attributes database so we will be able to provide increasingly accurate budgeting by timekeeper and task. The more our lawyers use budgets with JB task codes, the more useful this database will become for budgeting different types of matters.

Adding the value

Those who have used our team in the past are our largest repeat customers and are providing their clients with real-time transparency, accurate budgets and comparisons to actual time and disbursements incurred, as well as after-action reviews to go over lessons learned. Some lawyers use the PMO for one aspect such as tracking the progress of e-discovery; others use a more fulsome suite of the tools starting with milestones, dependencies, task lists, probability trees, budgets compared to time incurred, and after-action reviews. We were told that one of our clients using multiple law firms cited our firm's matter budgeting capabilities as the paradigm for all of the law firms working for that client, and that client required all of their outside law firms to conform to our model of tracking and presenting information. On another matter, the project management team's monthly estimates compared to actual time incurred varied by three to five percent from the actual results. For comparison, the lawyers previously performing this task were generating budgets which varied approximately 30 percent from budget. In addition to improving the accuracy, centralizing the PMO has helped with knowledge management by consolidating more of the matter budgets with one group and has also improved profitability by increasing visibility to all timekeepers and reducing amounts that lawyers are writing off before the clients get the bills.

Another benefit of the PMO and use of LPM on matters is increasing accountability for daily time entry and tracking of disbursements. Daily time entry helps us accurately measure the "cost" of performing individual tasks and reduces leakage. Using LPM on a matter requires that timekeepers enter their time to provide an accurate real-time picture of progress and time spent on tasks. Prompt time entry allows partners managing matters to course-correct throughout the month. It also allows our legal teams to provide the most accurate accruals to our clients before the firm's month-end close. In addition, LPM provides enhanced predictability for our lawyer teams and clients.

Our goal is to create broad demand among our lawyers so the information we retrieve will be reusable not only for repeat lawyer and client customers, but also across practice groups, and to help with alternative fee estimations and tracking. We are currently in the process of creating a more robust budgeting tool and developing a "what if" scenarios tool to help our lawyers understand the potential impact of changing various staff levels to predict profitability of matters. We strongly encourage our lawyers to partner with our PMO to help them with matter management.

As more and more matters require budgets and tracking against budgets, for fixed fee arrangements and for large matters where staffing can be hard to track, the value of using the PMO seems indisputable as well as inevitable. The greatest benefit of our approach is that it is not a one-size-fits all program, but rather, a menu of tools and customizable codes and taxonomies that our lawyers can embrace. I like to think we have built what Professor Clayton Christensen called sustaining technology[2] in his classic book, *The Innovator's Dilemma* (1997) – i.e. a technology and methodologies that improve performance. Culturally, taking this approach has fostered an important level of buy-in among our lawyers and clients, a healthy respect for the value of process, and the benefit that using LPM and those without legal credentials, but with financial and project management professional skills, can bring to matter management.

References

1. Also known as UTBMS codes. See LEDES.org.
2. Christensen, Clayton M. (1997) *The Innovator's Dilemma*, Introduction at xviii, Harper Business, New York.

Chapter 2: Innovations in legal project management – a law firm case study focusing on client needs

By Randall Brater and Katie Heilman, practicing lawyers at Arent Fox LLP

Introduction

The overarching goal of legal project management is to eliminate surprises. This includes surprises for clients when they receive an invoice; surprises for law firms when their realization takes a significant hit; and surprises for clients and law firms when they are wrong about the scope, intensity, duration – and thus the cost – of a matter.

Client satisfaction, work efficiency, effective communication, and high realization are goals that everyone can agree on. But how can a law firm achieve those goals? Education and training on project management issues are common; implementing project management techniques by changing attitudes, habits, and perceptions is difficult. Staying up to date on Continuing Legal Education courses on project management can only do so much. That is why one law firm decided to hire a consultant and launch a number of pilot projects that explored the possibilities that project management can offer.

These projects included (1) a client-facing initiative geared towards improved communication, efficiency, and realization; (2) an internal team project aimed at better understanding responsibility, scope, and leadership for certain tasks; and (3) development of an improved budgeting and timekeeper tracking system that includes buy-in from all timekeepers to improve time recording, workflow distribution, and management of resources.

The lessons learned from these initiatives improved internal and external communication, increased realization, led to greater client satisfaction, better management of the firm's resources and, in some cases, reduced stress and improved morale within the legal team. These initiatives should provide insight and concrete steps for other law firms and in-house legal teams to undertake similar programs that can improve efficiencies and client satisfaction.

Pilot program one: client interface project

Law firms are often faced with a similar quandary: they are selected as outside counsel, but the fee or rate structure requested by the client is not feasible, or the budget assumptions are significantly altered without being effectively communicated.

So, what are the options for the law firm? One is to endure endless write-offs to maintain the client relationship and hope that the volume of work makes up for the reduction in realization. However, this usually leads only to an endless cycle of bad realization. The law firm can also decide not to represent the client on such matters because realization is so poor. But there is another option – one that is often overlooked – which is to establish a dialogue with the client that explains the rationale for the increased scope of work and the resulting increase in fees. Pulling back the curtain will provide insight for improving efficiencies, coordination, and knowledge for the law firm and the client, and should lead to fewer write-offs because the client will be aware of *why* the law firm is undertaking certain work and *why* the budget assumptions may be inaccurate. It is important to undertake this dialogue with the client not only at the outset of a matter, but regularly and consistently throughout the engagement. The maxim typically holds true that the better a client is informed, the better the realization for the law firm!

To test this theory, the law firm in question conducted a client-facing pilot program to implement legal project management strategies. Such a program can involve any type of matter, but in this instance, we will discuss litigation involving a large corporate client. The goal of the pilot program was to determine if legal project management practices that involve both the law firm and the client would help improve realization and reduce write-offs.

The focus of this program was on establishing an effective line of communication and securing client input on the budget. At the outset of the matter, the firm attorneys held a kick-off meeting that included not only the team that would handle the matter, but also the client's in-house counsel and other client stakeholders. The goal of the kick-off meeting was to set expectations for the budget, define the scope and timing of various tasks, and clarify the responsibilities between the client and the firm for finishing and approving various tasks. The firm and in-house attorneys discussed their expectations about staffing and deadlines, confirmed the roles and responsibilities of the firm's litigation team members, and defined the anticipated scope of the firm's work on the matter. The firm and client also discussed a preliminary budget and the assumptions about anticipated work that led to specific estimates in the budget.

During the meeting, the client and the firm determined that the firm was not planning to focus sufficient energy on certain tasks that were more important to the client and, as a result, it was agreed that some resources were not being allocated appropriately. The client and the firm also found that the budget assumptions for specific phases of the case were not accurate and, as a result, the budget was not sufficient. The firm also learned more about the individuals and tasks that were more important for the client to achieve a successful outcome. This information, in turn, provided valuable institutional knowledge and insight into the budget process from the client's perspective. All of this information enabled the firm and their client to determine that the scope of work needed to change and, therefore, the budget for certain phases of the case was adjusted accordingly.

As a result of this new information, the firm shifted its strategy in the case. Had this important information not been communicated at the outset, the firm would have had to write off substantial fees, and the client relationship would have suffered. The client had a better understanding of the phases of the case, the tasks that needed to be performed, how much specific work was expected to cost, and when those costs were anticipated – but it was imperative to establish an open dialogue so all of those details could be communicated clearly. For the firm, the updated budget better reflected the client's expectations and was a match for the client's internal fee approval processes. In other words, because the client and firm offered more transparency into their inner workings, the client was much better informed about the upcoming tasks and fees to be incurred – all of this because of a short kick-off meeting among stakeholders.

As the matter progressed, the firm provided the client with reports on the budget, which accompanied the monthly invoice. They also held periodic status meetings with the client's in-house counsel to discuss the budget, usually on a quarterly basis. Depending on the client, these periodic meetings can be held more frequently and can include substantive discussions about the case and/or the strategy for achieving the best business outcome. During those periodic meetings, adjustments were made to staffing, team member roles and responsibilities, and the scope of the firm's work to account for changing needs in the case.

The kick-off meeting and ongoing communication enabled the client to have a better understanding of the budget and strategic choices made by the firm, while the firm had a better understanding of the client's business objectives, fee approval process, and overall expectations for the outcome of the matter, while increasing the realization rate.

Due to the favorable results on this project, the firm adopted the practice of holding kick-off and regular status meetings to discuss the budget, corresponding assumptions, and substantive issues related to other cases. A result was an uptick in realization on matters where these practices were instituted, and the clients all reported increased satisfaction with firm service.

Pilot program two: staffing/workflow project

There are many lawyers at law firms that are cognizant of the benefits of legal project management techniques, but assume their teams are functioning just fine without any need for interference. The mantra goes something like: "We've been practicing together for so long that we know each other's quirks and tendencies in and out."

But even the best and most profitable practices are subject to complacency, miscommunication, and an inability to recognize or adapt to changing circumstances. As a result, every team of lawyers can benefit from an inward look at how the team is functioning and an assessment of how each team member views their responsibilities as compared to the whole. The law firm in question therefore decided to conduct a pilot program on a well-functioning, successful practice. The program was aimed at using legal project management techniques to assess the team's management, morale, and responsibilities to improve internal staffing and workflow for work performed on a fixed-fee basis. In this program, a team of intellectual property attorneys and paralegals supporting a corporate client with a large portfolio participated in a two-day workshop to explore the use of legal project management practices to assess and improve the team's processes for managing the client's portfolio.

During the workshop, the team was asked to discuss and explore the responsibilities of each team member for the activity required to track the client's portfolio activity. In order to do so, the team used a "RASCI" analysis. Specifically, the team identified, for each task, the team member(s) **R**esponsible, **A**ccountable, **S**upportive, **C**onsulted, and/or **I**nformed. A more enhanced version of this analysis is now available for attorneys called a "LACI" analysis.[1] Under this type of analysis, lawyers can identify who is **L**eading, **A**ssisting, **C**onsulting, and **I**nformed. The goal of both of these analyses is to determine how the work is managed and to ensure, for example, that a particular task does not have two people assisting with no one leading, or vice versa.

In the workshop, the team developed an inventory of 14 charts to track the client's portfolio activity. The charts are used to manage the portfolio and provide status reports to the client. Through this exercise, the team discovered areas of overlap in team member responsibilities, minor gaps in coverage, and a lack of accountability for some tasks. Despite the fact the team was providing stellar advice and assistance to the client, they were able to identify areas of improvement to ensure the client's needs were handled in an even more exceptional manner. The exercise eliminated the possibility that certain tasks would go undone, uncompleted, or be delayed.

During the workshop, the team identified several focus areas to consider as they continue to identify ways to improve client satisfaction and cost-effectiveness within the fixed-fee framework. These included managing scope creep (the expansion of the agreed scope of work), maintaining the quality of the work in the face of increasing client demands and cost pressures, improving efficiency to preserve profitability, and reducing risk from uncertainty by unanticipated legal or factual issues.

The workshop provided a solid foundation for the team to build from in improving their internal processes for managing the client's portfolio. The workshop helped align individual members' understanding of team responsibilities and objectives, quickly addressed gaps in coverage, and improved accountability. The workshop resulted in the team developing a series of specific recommendations for improving internal processes, with the four focus areas discussed above in mind. These recommendations included streamlining the preparation of the 14 charts, developing standard templates or forms for routinely prepared documents, and exploring technology tools that may lead to increased efficiencies. Overall, the team was able to create efficiencies and reduce costs, which resulted in increased client satisfaction and a reduction in stress and improved morale within the team.

Pilot program three: internal budget and timekeeper tracking

Most lawyers understand the value of creating a budget. But many lawyers stop there – they create a static budget tailored to the client's needs or expectations and do not make appropriate adjustments to the budget and its assumptions over time. Even more importantly, lawyers can be notoriously bad at estimating the amount of time needed for associates and paraprofessionals to complete their tasks.

Creating a budget is therefore only the first step. The budget must become a dynamic document that is shared with the entire team *and* is tracked in real-time. But how do you accomplish this? In a third pilot program, the law firm discussed using legal project management practices to develop an internal budget and timekeeper system. This system has two components: a matter-specific budget tracking system, and a practice group level timekeeper tracking system.

The internal budget tracking system was developed by the firm's lawyers and accounting team and tracks hours billed and fees and costs incurred on large, complex matters. The system is used for internal tracking purposes and can be designed to interface with clients. Involving the accounting team is key – this way real-time hours can be tracked against the budget. Including the entire team – lawyers and paraprofessionals – in the process increases internal communication, leads to better and faster time entries, and can avoid the frustration of surprises when the draft invoices or pro formas are distributed.

The best way to create transparency into the time spent is to use appropriate phase and task codes. These may be modified depending on the needs of the case or the particular client. Either way, lawyers (and possibly clients) will know how the fees and costs are accruing as compared to the budget. This system provides a number of benefits, including an early warning system for cost overruns which allows lawyers to quickly understand changing assumptions about the scope or cost of a certain aspect of a case. As a result, the billing partner can receive budget updates in real-time and can communicate issues or concerns to the client before they get an invoice containing an unwanted suprise. The end result is higher realization, as the client has more insight into the invoices.

Once all of the timekeepers on matters are accustomed to real-time budget tracking, it becomes easier to ensure that time entries are done more expeditiously. And the same principles that apply to tracking budgets for client matters can be applied to managing firm resources. The data used to monitor and track client budgets was also used to create a practice group-centric timekeeper tracking system. The firm utilizes this system to track the time entries for attorneys and other timekeepers on a practice group level. The system tracks hours billed for attorneys and other timekeepers on a matter-by-matter basis, and distinguishes between billable and non-billable time. It also tracks the average amount of time it takes to enter and close time. The metrics derived from this system are provided to practice group leaders and managers on a weekly and monthly basis. This provides improved insight into the amount of time different timekeepers are devoting to various matters.

The data allows practice group leaders to improve the distribution of work among timekeepers and ensure that all of the firm's resources are being maximized.

The benefits of implementing this system have been considerable. The budget tracking system, which has been widely adopted by billing partners across the firm's offices, has promoted transparency and increased efficiency, and allowed the firm to better manage client expectations and eliminate surprise. Use of the timekeeper tracking system enables firm management to better track attorney productivity on a real-time basis, increases the likelihood of an even distribution of workflow, and provides an early warning system to address potential issues with attorney performance. Among these other benefits, the tracking system has improved realization, as timekeepers enter and close out time on a more contemporaneous basis.

Conclusion

Legal project management is more than a buzzword. When the firm took the initiative of exploring the use of legal project management techniques to advance the firm's business objectives, the firm quickly realized tangible and, in some cases, quantifiable benefits. The pilot programs described above and other similar initiatives developed as an outgrowth of these programs were not resource-intensive to implement and yet generated efficiencies, improved client relations, and increased realization. Legal project management is something firms and in-house legal departments managing complex matters in today's competitive and cost-sensitive legal market would be wise to consider.

Reference

1. Kleinman & Leventon, *Faster-Better-Cheaper Through Legal Project Management: The LACI Chart*, Bloomberg BNA, Corporate Accountability Report (June 2, 2016).

Chapter 3:

Putting legal project management principles into practice for M&As

By Byron Kalogerou, partner at McDermott Will & Emery LLP, and Dennis J White, senior counsel at Verrill Dana LLP

Introduction

Like most other theories, principles and operational methods, legal project management (LPM) sounds eminently logical and interesting at first hearing. However, the real power and effectiveness of LPM only become truly appreciated when LPM is put to work and applied to a particular matter. It is "where the rubber meets the road".

This chapter validates the truth of that idiom by demonstrating how LPM can significantly help lawyers in running M&A transactions more efficiently and effectively to deliver greater client satisfaction.

What is LPM? At base, it involves a disciplined approach to the practice of law using widely recognized management tools and techniques that can be applied to a wide range of practice areas. However, LPM is most impactful when those tools and techniques are tailored to a particular practice area, and within that area, to a specific type of project.

When initially introduced to LPM, a busy (and perhaps skeptical) lawyer is apt to say: "It generally sounds interesting and seems to make sense, but I need to understand how LPM will help me in my practice – and, by the way, don't take up a lot of my time in explaining it and implementing it."

Each of the authors of this chapter is a deal lawyer who has handled a large number of M&A transactions, large and small, across a wide range of industries and often around the world. Through that experience, each of us had become sold on the many benefits of using LPM in running deals, including: greater efficiency, reduced errors, better communication, fewer surprises, and satisfied clients. We also recognized that, with LPM, we were doing many of the things we had already done before, just more consciously and thoughtfully.

Our experience led us in 2012 to put on a panel presentation on the use of project management before the M&A Committee of the Business

Law Section of the American Bar Association. It was the first time LPM was openly discussed before the group. Our audience was comprised of experienced M&A lawyers. In all candor, their response was somewhat mixed. Some – mostly those who were already feeling pressure from clients to adopt LPM techniques – got what we were saying. Others who had never heard of LPM asked: "Why is this needed?" and "Why do I need to change the way I practice?"

Undaunted, we held the first meeting of a newly formed M&A Task Force on Legal Project Management in Mergers and Acquisitions a few months later. The Task Force ultimately grew to over 70 members, comprised of private law firm practitioners, in-house lawyers, corporate law department operations managers, academics, and consultants from around the world. Using project management practices ourselves, Aileen Leventon, a consultant and former M&A lawyer, served as project manager to the task force.

At the time we launched the Task Force, the literature on using LPM was largely general in nature. To our knowledge, there was (and still is) no other book that focuses solely on the use of LPM in M&A transactions.

M&A deals are different from other legal engagements in a number of ways:

- **Multiple lawyers involved**. Beyond the corporate lawyers who are running the deal, M&A transactions typically involve a large number of other legal specialists (e.g., tax, environmental law, ERISA, IP, employment law, etc.) that must be coordinated and managed. Their due diligence findings must be captured when it comes time to negotiate the acquisition agreement and handle post-closing integration.
- **Many other players**. In addition to the client's team, they can also involve a variety of advisors and professionals beyond the legal deal team (e.g., investment bankers, accountants, environmental engineers, etc.). Again, management and coordination are critical.
- **Fast-paced**. They are relatively fast-moving. While litigation can drag on for years, most M&A deals are closed in three to six months.
- **Often international**. They often involve different geographies (with different time zones, legal systems, languages and cultures).
- **Phase-based**. They proceed in distinct, though often overlapping, phases.
- **Business-driven**. Since they are directly driven by a business objective, clients are more likely to regard them as projects.

As a result, we concluded that M&A transactions had unique attributes that needed to be addressed with some particularity. While important in changing mindsets, general LPM concepts and principles, we concluded, did not constitute a complete answer. Even more importantly, we determined that we needed to be specific and use deal nomenclature if we hoped to gain acceptance and adoption by practicing M&A lawyers.

As a result, the Task Force decided to develop a set of tools that lawyers could utilize in leading and managing M&A transactions. The initial set of tools was collected in an ABA book entitled *Using Legal Project Management in Merger and Acquisition Transactions: A Guidebook for Managing Deals Efficiently and Effectively* (2016). A second edition of the book, with additional tools, was published in the spring of 2018.

In producing the guidebook, we were not seeking to establish standards of practice. Deal lawyers are free to search through the book's toolbox and use those they believe will be most helpful in a particular transaction. Since the tools are downloadable from the web, they can also be customized for the matter at hand. We also believed that such practical tools would be helpful to legal project managers and consultants who might not be deeply versed in M&A and who were trying to assist deal lawyers new to LPM.

Given that M&A deals proceed in distinct phases, we grouped the tools consistently with the distinct phases of a transaction: pre-deal, deal and post-deal. We also developed several tools for budgeting and billing M&A deals. The following are thumbnail descriptions of each of the tools included.

Pre-deal

Acquisition task checklist

This tool is the equivalent of a "pre-flight checklist" for an M&A deal. It is intended to help ensure that nothing falls through the cracks and that all the myriad tasks associated with a typical M&A transaction are covered and coordinated.

Initial deal scoping discussion

This tool provides a script for an early stage conversation between the client and law firm regarding important background information on the transaction (e.g., deal structure, industry, business objectives, and timing), key issues likely to arise, and the scope of work to be undertaken by the law firm. It aids the client and the law firm in organizing and coordinating their respective responsibilities.

Confirmation of deal scope

Law firms ask clients to sign engagement letters all the time. However, apart from some boilerplate, these letters focus principally on billing rates and fee arrangements and speak in only the most general terms about what is expected of the law firm or the client. This tool develops a formal scoping letter on a standalone basis or as an addendum to an engagement letter, detailing what the law firm is expected to do and, just as important, what the law firm is not expected to do.

Deal management discussion outline

This outline of a conversation between the client and the law firm addresses how the deal will be run (e.g., confidentiality concerns, communication protocols, other advisors who are involved, risk factors, closing mechanics, and post-closing integration issues).

Deal counsel compact

This tool is a checklist of principles and guidelines that the parties may jointly adopt at the outset of the transaction to promote a higher degree of collaboration among all parties. These suggested rules of engagement between opposing counsel are intended to avoid confusion, reduce friction, and streamline the deal-making process.

Deal kick-off meeting checklist

This tool provides a checklist for an initial all hands/all parties meeting to address communication and negotiation protocols. A staple used by investment bankers in initial public offerings and other financings, the kick-off meeting checklist provides an opportunity for key players and their legal counsel to set the agenda for the deal and discuss background, structure, deal documents, timetables, and communication protocols.

Early due diligence assessment

This tool can be used to prioritize the due diligence effort by initially focusing on matters of client concern with the objective of better managing the time and expense of the due diligence process. This approach breaks down due diligence into stages and can streamline the overall due diligence process when an initial review identifies areas of serious concern that might result in abandoning the transaction.

Multi-jurisdictional transaction checklist

This tool is a checklist of issues to consider in an M&A transaction that is multi-jurisdictional in nature. For example, buyer and seller may be headquartered in different countries, or the seller may maintain operations in multiple jurisdictions.

Carveout transaction checklist

A carveout transaction involves the sale of a subsidiary, division or business unit where the seller continues in existence as an operating entity following the closing. Carveout transactions are complex and raise their own unique set of issues. This internal tool is intended to assist counsel and client in planning and handling such a transaction.

Deal phase

Deal issues drafting guide

This tool sets forth a list of issues that counsel and client may want to consider and address at an early stage in establishing negotiating positions and drafting a purchase agreement. It is intended to serve as an internal tool, not to be shared with opposing counsel.

Deal issues negotiating tool

This tool is intended to highlight and facilitate the negotiation of significant issues early in the process. Typically, many key issues such as baskets, caps, and other indemnification terms are not reflected in a letter of intent, but are instead negotiated piecemeal or through the exchange of multiple drafts of the deal documents. With this tool, counsel and client can exchange proposals with their counterparts and attempt to crystallize the more significant deal issues at an early stage.

Roles and responsibilities chart (leading/assisting/consulted/informed)

This chart assigns and tracks the specific roles and responsibilities of individual members of the deal team. The purpose of the chart is to designate those who will be accountable, ensure others are kept in the loop and positioned to provide useful input, and avoid duplication of work because of lack of clarity regarding roles.

Task status report

This tool sets out a template of a report to communicate the current status of the various tasks that are necessary to close an M&A transaction. Sometimes called an "information radiator," it is intended to provide progress updates on the status of various key tasks.

Post-closing phase

Post-matter assessment

Post-matter debriefings focus on lessons learned and enable the law firm and client to capture knowledge and improve processes by considering what went right, what went wrong, and what might be improved. Checklists guide the counsel and client through the assessment process.

Post-acquisition transaction checklist

While deal making is hard, integration is even more difficult. The projected values to be realized from an acquisition are often lost on integration. This tool provides a list of questions and action items for a buyer to consider in developing and implementing a post-closing integration plan.

Billing/budgeting tools

M&A codes

This tool provides a set of codes for budgeting purposes and reporting time incurred by law firms in M&A transactions. The codes reflect the phases of a transaction, rather than deal tasks, and report the involvement of subject matter experts who support the transaction. They have been adopted by LEDES.org and are described in detail in a book co-authored by the project managers of the LPM task force, Aileen Leventon and Jenny Anne Horst-Martz, *Best Practices for Using UTBMS Codes in M&A Transactions* (2016).

Alternative M&A fee arrangements

While alternative fee structures are often used in litigation matters, clients and law firms frequently struggle in attempting to adopt alternative fee structures for M&A deals to better align their respective interests. This tool sets forth a menu of such alternative fee structures.

Deal magnitude and complexity tool

This tool identifies certain elements of complexity that can consume resources, drive up legal costs and lengthen the duration in an M&A transaction. The elements appear in a matrix in which numerical points in increasing amounts are assigned as the magnitude and complexity of each element increases. Consideration of such elements is critical in gathering the resources, preparing a budget, and setting expectations for a M&A deal.

M&A budgeting tool

Many lawyers do not know where to begin when a client asks for a fee budget for a M&A transaction. Utilizing the M&A codes referred to above, this Excel-based tool sets out deal phases and allows counsel to insert tasks, estimated hours to complete the tasks, and timekeepers by seniority. With the estimated hours and billing rate inserted, counsel can calculate a budget with a reasonable degree of precision.

Conclusion

Our experience with the Task Force and producing the guidebook has led us to conclude that, irrespective of the practice area involved, detailed legal project management tools like these can drive efficiency, accountability and predictability.

To be effective and to foster adoption by practicing lawyers, LPM tools and techniques should be tailored to the particular practice area – whether it be M&A, trial, or regulatory. By necessity, they must be fairly detailed. General LPM principles can only take you so far. Once LPM tools have been developed for the practice area, they should be further refined for the specific project at hand. Finally, they need to be logically arranged, and relatively simple to understand and easy to implement.

Chapter 4:

Innovations in professional development for legal project development skills

By adjunct associate professor Todd Hutchison, chair of the International Institute of Legal Project Management

Sustainable legal practice relies on the expertise of its lawyers and their ability to attract and retain clients. This calls for skills beyond their knowledge of the law: to the need to be better communicators, more technologically savvy, and having enhanced interpersonal skills.

Advances in adult education to better prepare the modern attorney is seeing more flexible modes of structured learning, global training options, and a greater use of technology. The focus is not simply on law; it expands to integrating legal knowledge and non-legal skills that enables lawyers to work better with people, and technology that makes a difference to their effectiveness in the workplace.

Legal project management skill areas

A global study conducted by the International Institute of Legal Project Management[1] of lawyers applying legal project management from nine different countries found that LPM skills went beyond simply project management practices to include technology, process mapping, and leadership skills. This is why project management as a discipline is often referred to as an art and a science, as it combines both interpersonal skills with the complexity of process-driven practice management expertise.

Often referred to as soft skills, improving interpersonal competence is important for dealing with the need for productive networking that leads to work engagements, improved leadership of legal teams, and more effective communication with clients, particularly those dealing with highly emotionally-driven legal matters, such as the stresses of litigation and family law. This extends to emotional intelligence, where an attorney develops greater resilience to deal with the daily stresses of legal work, and their ability to better control their own emotional state and in dealing more professionally with others.

Law schools shift to technology-enabled education

Due to technological advances, the profession is changing. The growth of this change is hastening as technology drives the behaviors of both lawyers and the increasingly internet-savvy client, who have far more information on handheld devices than ever before. This impacts their day-to-day decisions and their likely perceived need for engaging professional legal services.

Consider technology's impact on undergraduate law degree studies, with the transition from their historic physical presence in university libraries that have now been replaced with impressive online resources, rendering the libraries far less relevant. Even law schools have progressed from pure face-to-face education delivery to models which include complete online delivery models.

Technology has even facilitated the use of real-time webcast-based options, where students have global access to live law-school classes and tutorials from anywhere in the world. Figure 1 shows lawyer Anna Marra FIILPM at the Spanish IE Law School conducting legal project management training in a virtual classroom environment. This has allowed the university to teach a wider cohort beyond its homeland Spain.

Figure 1: IE Wow Room – university virtual classroom (Photo courtesy of IE)

A student in one country can study for a law degree in a completely different land, and a resident law student can go traveling around the world whilst still progressing their home-based university studies. This has also allowed others wishing to progress their legal studies while continuing full-time employment. Practicing attorneys who may be more inclined to undertake specialist postgraduate training from the comfort of their own offices now have a plethora of opportunities. This is deemed to be more time-effective, and enables a learner to be more in control of their schedule and educational pathway. This new revolution offers study at any time, in any place and on any device.

Recognizing legal project management competency

Law schools in universities like Swansea University (UK), IE Law School (Spain), and Pontificia Universidad Católica de Valparaíso de Chile (Chile) are leading legal project management education. They are integrating their law studies with professional global certification from the International Institute of Legal Project Management, giving their students practice-ready recognition.

Global certification in legal project management and the accreditation of LPM programs aims to ensure standardized practices worldwide are shaping consistent best practice and lawyers can gain third-party recognition for their education and workplace experiences. Qualifications can be accelerated through recognized prior learning and advanced standing options which recognize workplace experience.

Face-to-face education comes with the important interaction, engagement, and the ability to ask questions in person. This is where real-time online education can be useful even when physical presence is not possible. Although face-to-face training remains the preferred teaching method, continuing legal education now presents global options from online and blended teaching modes for short courses, postgraduate studies and now international LPM certification.[2] Global LPM certification aimed at legal team members like the Legal Project Associate™ (LPA), and for the legal project manager like the Legal Project Practitioner™ (LPP), sets a worldwide standard to recognize those trained in and practicing LPM.

Globalization and a transition to online learning

Online education has even opened up opportunities for practicing lawyers to be accredited in other countries, such as a non-USA based lawyer who is now entitled to sit for a US Bar exam and become a US attorney.[3]

Training programs from law schools are even being offered at no charge and being made available internationally, with the hope of capturing new students or ultimately receiving payment where a student later seeks a certificate to validate their learning experience. The introduction of Massive Open Online Courses (MOOCs) has offered free online legal course access even from leading universities like Yale University, the University of Chicago and the University of Pennsylvania.[4] MOOC programs can also lead to an innovative model of micro-credentialing, which is a form of mini-degree or certification, that now includes MicroMaster programs for graduate lawyers leading to master degree level qualifications.

Expanding from law to business knowledge

Legal project management skills have enabled attorneys to extend their competency to more business knowledge, as every business runs projects, and understanding the wider project management discipline gives more insights to the challenges of the organization's own project practices. This particularly helps the in-house counsel member to be better involved in the business due to their expertise in how projects are correctly planned and executed, and recognizes that oversee process improvement projects for their own portfolio, such as implementing practice management software. The acknowledgement that anything new, unique or significant are all likely to be "projects" brings the understanding that project management is a key knowledge area for any leader.

Engaging external legal counsel on assignments means that in-house counsel have to be cognizant of managing the legal spend on behalf of the business, and that is where fixed price and other alternate fee arrangements have helped maintain their budgets. This shift away from the billable hour has been one of the key drivers for legal project management implementation.

Given all strategy is implemented through projects, LPM competency also better equips those lawyers residing on boards of management with increased insights about the execution of strategy. The understanding of the practices of risk, and lessons learnt, as well as issues and change management, ensures greater governance oversight. These are covered in the online course offered by the International Institute of Legal Project Management.[6]

Artificial intelligence and technology-driven legal practice

Technological innovation is also making the client more legal-savvy. With the advent of the internet, there has been a shift from the lawyer being the key source of legal advice. Readily available online legal guidance to the layperson, and the ease of getting limited legal education and insights without attorney intervention has emerged. This extends to the growing use of artificial intelligence that has facilitated the use of virtual legal information resource assistants like Ailira,[7] which provides consumer legal advice on diverse legal matters from wills to business structuring and asset protection; it is even able to generate fully certified wills. This extends to virtual lawyers like those being developed by Ross Intelligence[8] that are helping with legal research, workflow efficiencies and preparation of legal advice. These systems can even be asked legal questions directly in natural language, mimicking a human interaction.

The argument for providing low-cost and often free sources of legal guidance is to provide everyone with access to affordable legal advice, and to provide improved tools to lawyers to deliver better and faster services. An article in *Forbes* magazine[9] noted that emerging technologies can enhance the legal services to clients. TechCrunch reported back in 2015 that the market size for legal research software was valued at approximately US$8.4B[10] annually. The vision of a "law firm full of technology-turbocharged lawyers"[11] is also underway in Silicon Valley through a legal start-up law firm called Atrium. Software has become a key factor in providing streamlined legal services. Whilst alternate fee arrangements recognize that client fees can be matched to the value legal services offer, the use of software has its advantages, as profit can still be made with a higher reliance on attorneys leveraging software applications.

Whilst it is not proposed that artificial intelligence replaces the lawyer, it does suggest that the modern lawyer needs to work smarter in adapting to, and leveraging, technology in their ability to deliver legal matters more efficiently whilst maintaining the highest level of quality. In 2016, McKinsey estimated 22 percent of work done by lawyers and 35 percent by law clerks could be automated,[12] notwithstanding any new roles that will be added to the law profession to compensate the changing landscape. Susskind (2017)[13] envisages ten future roles for lawyers that vary from a legal process analyst to a legal risk manager. Like all evolution, it requires adaption, and education enables change.

Influx of non-attorney project managers into legal practice

With the introduction into law practices of project professionals who are not lawyers serving as legal project managers shows a growing model of integrating less expensive personnel to help guide the process of legal matters. This arises out of the argument that "the non-lawyer who does the role will be more efficient, motivated and willing to challenge the status quo, because their motivation is in doing things better/quicker/cheaper, not getting legal experience."[14] This effectively allows the legal project manager to focus on the process, and the legal practitioner on the law tasks at hand, and at the same time reducing the cost of the legal project team. This calls for education programs to learn the theory of business law to enhance the non-lawyer LPM legal knowledge without training them to become legal practitioners,[15] although determining the level of legal education may present challenges in itself.

Independent of being a qualified attorney or professional project manager, the legal project manager's educational requirements need to focus on professional skills, technical skills and the critical soft skills. This includes understanding what innovation in technology will aid greater efficiency in the workplace, and the importance of understanding how to change and integrate current systems and processes with new technology and differing ways of working. The workforce is now including options of outsourcing legal work to less expensive service providers, and virtual teams geographically spread. This all calls for managing partners to change their mindset to enable a modification to traditional practices, pushing against a profession that has traditionally been wary of change.

Alternate fee arrangements impacting the ways of working

The traditional billable hour can lend itself to less productive work, as the longer the work takes, the more profit is achieved. In psychology, this is called a "secondary gain", meaning a benefit that keeps a lawyer less productive than their actual capability. The billable model is largely based on using more labor that returns greater revenue, but not necessarily more value for the client.

Where a fixed price model is implemented, the driver for efficiency is increased, as the faster the work is completed, and the less physical labor resources used, the greater the profit. This assumes the quality of the legal output is not compromised, and the efficiencies come from leveraging corporate information, technology use, and more personal productivity. This suggests time management skills may now be of greater demand, and health and wellness programs to balance the pressures of the work.

The Parkinson's Law principle of "work expands to fill the time available for its completion" suggests that if you gave a legal team three days to do two days of work, the productivity may be decreased, and may lead to three days of effort, effectively increasing the cost and the delivery schedule.

Compare the efficiency of a lawyer working on the day before their annual leave compared to a normal day in the office. The time criticality usually leads to less breaks, less talking, and more focused effort. It could be then argued that the billable hour could have led to lower performance that has become the norm, with aging soon-to-retire partners trying to stall with technology improvements to avoid having to learn more and adapt their own practices.

Productivity in each hour, as opposed to working longer hours, is what smart working promotes and LPM practices aim to achieve. Looking toward ways of greater leadership, emotional intelligence of building self-awareness and maintaining self-wellness, as well as refined interpersonal skills for more effective communications with others, all leads to a more satisfying career.

Lifelong adult learning

In studying the complexity of the human being shows that an individual's uniqueness is based on four influences, divided up between the nature and nurture phenomenon that reflects what we are born with (and later adapt) and what life conditioning brings.

The nature elements relate to a person's core behavioral style and their communication style, and the differences in those explain why learning needs to cater for those who learnt better from watching (visual learners), listening (auditory learners) or practicing (kinesthetic learners). The nurture elements relate to a person's personal knowledge and expertise, and their values and belief systems. The values and belief systems include the influences of religious, culture, language, personal thinking and attitude. Values and belief systems end up being a primary factor to human interaction and personal drive.

Evidence in the research of learning has shown that a traditional career path may limit learning from lack of new thinking,[16] and that adapting to new roles, new technologies and workplace changes can build flexibility and learning agility. When developed, it leads to a law firm culture that remains innovative and helps sustain competitive edge.[17] This is the essence of the introduction to legal project management, as it is calling for new thinking, learning and ongoing professional development. It challenges the existing work paradigms and brings out innovative thinking to drive change that can bring a law firm into a new state of operation and competitiveness.

Maintaining learning therefore is a part of progress, and this explains why aged managing partners who avoid technology may be inadvertently setting their practices up to fail when they retire. Understanding the benefits of learning cannot be understated.

Innovation and interactive education delivery

Innovations in e-learning is now seeing more learner-machine interaction; gamification design that sets up a more competitive, interactive and engaging environment; and assessments that then adapt the learning pathway to suit their educational needs. Where low comprehension on a topic is detected, the computer is routed to provide more education, and where the student is accelerating, they are directed through to more advanced knowledge. The student is educated effectively based on their gaps in learning, and the experience altered to meet their specific needs.

Online video platforms like YouTube have proven education is wanted in smaller chunks of high relevant content over longer videos. Time for education is often limited in a world of information overload, and therefore current e-learning design is favoring shorter duration segment-based videos that keep the viewer intensively interested.

Robots like the NAO from Softbank Robotics – who have more than 10,000 humanoid robots in the marketplace as interactive companions – that can chat in more than 20 languages are already being used in schools and universities. Ross Intelligence artificial intelligence have been focused on the legal profession and building tools to enhance the attorney's abilities.[19]

The attorney of the future

Looking toward the future of professional development, the rapid advances in artificial intelligence will bring integration of existing and further developed technologies to the legal learning development. Robots are already able to learn from human interactions and respond in adaptive ways, including adding banter in their interactions. This will lead to virtual simulated learning environments that mimic courtrooms through wearable technologies, with robotic interactions based on natural language with customized responses from artificial intelligence that will create a totally unique learning experience. This would enable simulated life-like legal matters to be executed in a virtual world to allow workplace-based practice training towards building and refining attorney's knowledge and potentially testing arguments and practicing delivery.

The future attorney will be dependent on knowing and utilizing technology, and legal matters will continue to be projects and need ever-increasingly skilled legal project managers.

References

1. IILPM (2017) Legal Project management Competency Framework, A Global Standard for Professional Development in Legal Project Management, Executive Summary, International Institute of Legal Project Management.
2. IILPM (2018) International Legal PM Certification, International Institute of Legal Project Management, URLhttp://www.iilpm.com/#certification.
3. The College of Law (2018) Practicing in the USA, The College of Law (Australia), URL: https://www.collaw.edu.au/learn-with-us/practising-in-the-usa, Date sighted 15 September 2018.
4. MOOC (2018) Law MOOCs and Free Online Courses, Massive Open Online Course, URL: https://www.mooc-list.com/tags/law.
5. MOOC (2018) International Law, MicroMaster Program Details, Massive Open Online Course, eDx, URL: https://www.edx.org/micromasters/louvainx-international-law.
6. See https://www.iilpm.com/#elearning.
7. Marks, L (2017) *Artifical Intelligence Law Firm Aims to Rollout in Remote Low Socio-economic Communities*, Australian Broadcast Corporation, URL: http://www.abc.net.au/news/2017-11-13/artificial-intelligence-law-firm-without-lawyers-in-darwin/9146332
8. Ross (2018) On-Demand Research Associate, Ross Intelligence, URL: http://www.rossintelligence.com/.
9. Chowdhry, A (2016) Law Firm BakerHostetler Hires a 'Digital Attorney' Named ROSS, *Forbes*, May 17 2016, URL: https://www.forbes.com/sites/amitchowdhry/2016/05/17/law-firm-bakerhostetler-hires-a-digital-attorney-named-ross/#61d5a76478c4
10. Cutler, K (2015) YC's Ross Intelligence Leverages IBM'S Watson to Make Sense of Legal Knowledge, *TechCrunch*, July 20 2015, URL: https://techcrunch.com/2015/07/27/ross-intelligence/.
11. Dwoskin, E (2017) This Silicon Valley Start-up Wants to Replace Lawyers with Robots, *Washington Post*, URL: https://www.washingtonpost.com/news/innovations/wp/2017/09/14/this-silicon-valley-startup-wants-to-replace-lawyers-with-robots/?noredirect=on&utm_term=.f12732cf445b.
12. Winick, E (2017) Lawyer-Bots Are Shaking Up Jobs, *MIT Technology Review*, Dec 12 2017, URL: https://www.technologyreview.com/s/609556/lawyer-bots-are-shaking-up-jobs/

13. Susskind, R (2017) *Tomorrow's Lawyers – An Introduction to Your Future*, Oxford University Press, 2nd Edition.
14. Pennington, J (2016) *Developing and Keeping Specialist Legal Project Managers Within Law Firms*, URL: http://www.penningtonhennessy.com/blog/. developing-and-keeping-specialist-legal-project-managers-within-law-firms
15. Morris, R (2010) The Teaching of Law to Non-lawyers: An Exploration of Some Curriculum Design Challenges, *International Journal of Law in the Build Environment*, Vol. 2, Issue 3., pp. 232-245.
16. Janand, A (2018) *Learning on the Move: A Reassessment of Mobility Through the Lens of Bateson's Learning Theory*, Emerald Publishing Limited.
17. Coakes, E, Bradburn, A and Sugden, G (2004) Managing and Leveraging Knowledge for Organisational Advantage, *Knowledge Management Research and Practice*, Vol. 2 No. 2.
18. SoftBank (2018) *Find Out More About NAO*, SoftBank Robotics, URL : https://www.softbankrobotics.com/emea/en/robots/nao/find-out-more-about-nao.
19. ROSS (2018) Mission and Vision, Ross Intelligence. URL: https://rossintelligence.com/about/.

Chapter 5:
Daily management – meetings that matter

By Thomas Agostinelli, director of practice management at Butler Snow LLP

Not all meetings are a waste of time

How can meetings be synonymous with innovation, you may ask? This chapter intends to answer that question by exploring a disciplined approach to maximize effectiveness of legal project management (LPM) through daily meetings. These are also referred to as stand-ups, check-ins, huddles, or daily scrums, depending on the industry.

We recognize law firm and legal department calendars are littered with meetings, so why add more? Well, we find inspiration by exploring other industries who are both innovative and committed to consistent management. Agriculture, healthcare, and manufacturing – just to name a few – all share a common theme of tremendous innovation and fast-paced technological advancement in concert with simple daily management. Organizations often gain the largest impact by innovating through simplicity. Let us take a quick look at how each industry maximizes the effectiveness of their operation through daily management.

Agriculture

Agriculture has come a long way from the days of horse and plough. Farms now utilize GPS technology in self-driving tractors for variable rate application, with precision accuracy based on field location. In simple terms, farmers reduce costs by applying pesticides or fertilizer only where needed. Even with this level of sophistication, farmers continue to meet with their field hands at the barn each morning to discuss yesterday's progress and lay out today's plan. These daily gatherings cover items such as field completion and time remaining, proper application of inputs, and equipment maintenance.

Learn from thy neighbor

Two neighboring farmers were having a conversation at the turn row. One farmer, Jim, always admired his neighbor. Each year, he planted and harvested his crop on time. His fields were clean of weeds, and more importantly, his yields exceeded those of Jim's. With some frustration in his voice, Jim asked, "What's your secret? We have the same land, plant the same seeds, use the same equipment, and yet you have a better harvest. And, you go home each evening before me." His neighbor politely asked, "Jim, do you know what's the single most important thing for a crop?" Jim shook his head, "No, what?" His neighbor smiled, pointed to the ground and said, "To see your shadow."

Each morning, as Jim drank coffee at the local parts and supply store and caught up on the latest town news, his neighbor met with his work hands to set forth the day's plan. All the while, Jim's crew was left to make decisions independently, leading to inefficiencies.

Healthcare

Advancements in medicine and surgical procedures have not replaced the need for daily communication, but instead amplified it. Hospitals around the world have adopted a daily management methodology to improve both quality and speed of delivery for their patients. A primary goal is to reduce length of stay while providing the highest quality of care possible and preventing readmissions. As part of their continuous improvement programs, medical staff meet in front of storyboards with charts and graphs each day to discuss key metrics, also referred to as key process indicators (KPI) which may include patient wait times, laboratory cycle times, infection rates, etc.

Manufacturing

Similar to the examples already mentioned, daily production meetings in manufacturing are the norm. Daily stand-ups are built upon standardization which is one of the LEAN Management System foundations, promoting efficiency and continuous improvement through iterations and eliminating waste. Teams will typically meet on the manufacturing floor close to the production area to discuss metrics ranging from quality defect trends to inventory levels (e.g. finished goods or work in process) to on-time product delivery.

Daily management overcomes organizational deficiencies

In the early 2000s, I was a young engineer working for an electronics manufacturer. We employed a 7:15 AM daily stand-up meeting, where each supervisor reported yesterday's progress, today's goals, and any obstacles affecting desired outcomes. We were a high-tech PCB design and manufacturing company, yet we stood in front of a large whiteboard to plan and execute daily activities for hundreds of products, people and complex machinery every day. I questioned our sophistication until, one day, a Fortune 500 telecom client visited our company to perform an in-depth supply chain audit of our entire operation. After a two-week deep dive, we met with the auditors to discuss the results. We scored in the 60th percentile. The auditors stated, "Quite frankly, when our suppliers score below 70, we recommend replacing them. However, your organization does something better than any facility we have audited. Your commitment to a daily management system (DMS) is impressive." The story ended well, as we mitigated the gaps and later scored in the 90th percentile. Of course, we continued practicing our daily stand-up meetings, and from that day forward, I have been a firm believer in the effectiveness of the DMS.

These industries are a representative sample of the power of daily management, identifying what is critical to success and reviewing it with their respective teams. Organizations who are not utilizing this approach are missing an opportunity to improve their performance with minimum investment.

Why should law firms or legal departments be any different?

When to implement daily management

Do you have a team of people?

Daily stand-up meetings are not for every situation. Firms and legal departments need to identify when these meetings are beneficial. For example, small teams (three to four people) in close proximity develop a natural communication style that occurs throughout the day. These teams may not find daily stand-up meetings beneficial, unless the team members are disorganized.

However, as practice units or legal matters grow, communication tends to break down. Attorneys, secretaries and paralegals begin to recognize redundant or unnecessary work is being performed (often too late) because communication and priority are no longer timely or disseminated to all participants. More timekeepers are added to the file that may not have been part of the original budget. The opportunity for interaction and feedback from all team members is missing from the equation. As teams grow, daily meetings become more relevant to set the day's strategy and to understand who is doing the work.

Do you have a common purpose?
Daily meetings are built around a team of individuals who share a common purpose, whether it is a particular matter or a functional area within the department. Without commonality, the effort will be disjointed as each team member is focused on unrelated tasks.

Do you have matter plans?
Paraphrased from Lewis Carroll's *Alice's Adventures in Wonderland*, "If you don't know where you are going, any road will take you there". Matter plans with work breakdown structures identify phases, tasks, resources and due dates. Tracking these daily can be effective in maximizing profitability of the matter.

Do you have a large case? Or portfolio of matters?
When attorneys and paralegals are attempting to manage multiple matters at once or large complex matters with many moving parts, the need for daily meetings becomes more prevalent. Time is of the essence as attorneys are juggling various deadlines. The team can no longer afford a day lost focusing on the wrong task. Deviations from the original matter plan are not uncommon as the case progresses and new issues are discovered. New challenges arise by the hour in some instances. A daily alignment of effort helps avoid stressful moments and frustration of applying hours to low priority or no-longer-needed work product.

Do you have defined goals? Expected results?
Teams should have well-established goals, metrics and expectations to report progress and determine next steps. The measurement of success is better if broken down into smaller parts for easier consumption.

Do you have repetitive processes?
This is certainly not a requirement, but teams with consistent routines and work product will find identifying what to measure and track each day much easier than teams who have long-term deadlines and phases. Metrics take on many shapes and sizes, such as number of medical reviews in a litigation matter or contracts reviewed during due diligence.

However, this should not deter a team with more lengthy deadlines from daily meetings, as lack of progress – if not detected early enough – will place the team significantly behind schedule.

Do you have a defined pace of progress? Is it daily or weekly?

Pace matters, whether litigation is in full swing or the closing date is quickly approaching. When moving fast and changing day to day, conducting quick daily meetings becomes even more critical to success. When teams meet weekly, your project moves at a weekly pace. If you meet daily, you move at a daily pace. Ask yourself: how fast do you want to go?

Are you working under an alternative fee arrangement (AFA)?

Possibly more important than any of the items mentioned so far, a non-hourly fee arrangement (e.g. flat, fixed, contingency, etc.) is where legal project management techniques become critical, and daily meetings are a great tool to help manage every aspect of the matter, including staffing, task assignment, status, and results.

Benefits which reach beyond the meeting

Now that we have established when a team should initiate daily stand-up meetings, let's discuss the benefits – some more obvious than others.

Prioritization

Firstly, if the meeting is conducted effectively, it should only last 10-15 minutes. This forces the team to focus on the most important items of the day and drives a metric-centric approach. Each team member leaves understanding his or her priorities. There is no need for status email strings that go back and forth for hours filling up your inbox and distracting you from your work. Similarly, managers or team leads save time from having to walk around from office to office to get updates from their team and establish priorities.

Cost savings

Organizations who deploy daily stand-ups will report a higher level of engagement and less complaints about communication. With team members on the same page, the chance of redundant or unnecessary work is also reduced significantly (i.e. write-downs or write-offs). Progress is reported each day, so priorities are relevant and timely compared to meeting once a week (or not at all) where things can change significantly between meetings. Undesirable results or deviation from standard performance is easily detected and addressed.

Consistency

Organizations who deploy daily stand-up meetings will often reference the routine and rhythm it creates. When held at the beginning of each day, team members find comfort in a normal starting point. Early meetings also require team members to be present whether by phone or in the meeting room. As a side benefit, this will expose tardiness and absenteeism, which negatively affects team performance. Because each team member is required to report progress, they must be prepared. Lack of organization will also be exposed by this format. Not only are you creating accountability, you are creating awareness of what each team member is contributing to the whole.

Regarding rhythm, daily meetings create a daily pace. Teams begin to better understand their capabilities and what can truly be accomplished in a work day. Once a standard is established, the team is challenged to improve upon it.

Continuous improvement

Next, there is the benefit of continuous improvement. Reviewing metrics and trends each day creates the opportunity for teams to instantly see where improvements need to be made. Although this meeting is not intended for in depth problem solving, identifying a problem early allows team members the opportunity to address before it becomes a bigger issue.

Team building

One very important aspect is the amount of trust created among the team. Just through simple, consistent interaction, the team will grow respect for each other and develop trust that will allow them to perform at a much higher level.

Stand-up meetings in a law firm

A firm was involved in a multi-year, complex litigation requiring a large legal staff and many attorneys to support the effort, not to mention co-counsel, third-party vendors and the client. The internal team was organized by functions and phases of the litigation, with most team members specialized in their roles.

A small group of designated lead attorneys and lead paralegals provided oversight. The organizational model created silos among team members who focused only on their piece of the litigation. Pressure was placed on the team leads to "connect the dots" and "bridge communication".

Most communication occurred over emails including status updates. As the litigation grew, the stress on this management system compounded, and communication breakdowns became more frequent. And then one day, a lead paralegal resigned which magnified the issues. The departure created a perfect opportunity to introduce stand-up meetings. The format involved a representative from each functional area of the litigation facilitated by a manager. They met in front of a whiteboard. Each participant was given an opportunity to report recent accomplishments, next steps and any challenges to accomplish their goals. Initial meetings were filled with doubt and tension among the attendees. They harbored frustration towards each other from past mishaps or miscommunications. As each participant explained their challenges, their peers began to respect and appreciate each other. They offered to share workload and provide ideas on how to solve issues they had tackled in the past. They all gained an understanding of the big picture and not just what's happening in their area and how some of their decisions created difficulties for others. Sympathy and collaboration replaced frustration and fear. And most importantly, they began to develop trust. Not to mention, the actual performance of the team improved even as the litigation continued to grow and introduced new challenges.

Professional development

And finally, these meetings will offer an opportunity for coaching and mentoring. As team members struggle with various challenges, there is a good chance their peers have experienced a similar issue in the past and can provide advice on how to address it. In some instances, understanding what challenges one team member is facing exposes that other team members are creating those challenges and did not even realize it (i.e. actions affecting downstream processes).

Conducting efficient daily meetings

Great! The decision has been made to conduct daily meetings, so where do you start?

Attendees

The ideal meeting size is between five and 10, with no more than 15. If your meeting has more than 10 attendees, it is likely that some will have a passive role and not provide updates. The main qualification for attendance is that each member is responsible for task(s) in the matter plan, represents a central function to the execution of the matter or owns a process in the value stream. For example, consider the typical phases and tasks of a litigation matter plan. The meeting may have representatives from document review, litigation support, depositions, pleadings, witnesses, and trial prep in attendance. In many instances, the facilitator will add or remove attendees as the matters progress.

Facilitator

Speaking of the facilitator, the meeting must have a designated facilitator to keep the attendees on track and on time. The facilitator will start the meeting promptly and will call on attendees in an orderly fashion for status updates. The facilitator is responsible for identifying issues for the "parking lot", which will be discussed later. The facilitator will disseminate any notes from the meeting, which allows the attendees to share with other members who did not attend.

It is also important that this person create a productive and positive environment, treating failure not as a crime, but as an opportunity to learn from mistakes. The facilitator will encourage honest feedback and healthy conflict to resolve issues. Understanding these responsibilities, it is important that the team chooses their facilitator wisely.

Rules of engagement

Meeting expectations and consistency shall be established early. It is important that participants respect the meeting.

All meetings start on time even if attendees are late. End meetings on time as well, even if the facilitator must politely cut participants short on their updates. Explain to the team that it is their responsibility to develop a concise report out, two to three minutes and no more. Do not become discouraged. If they have never experienced this type of meeting, it will take some time for them to adjust, but they will soon come to appreciate the brevity.

Record and track progress. Whether metric-driven for repeatable activities or task driven from the matter plan, the team needs to show progress and be held accountable; otherwise, the purpose of the meeting is lost and is viewed as a waste of time. Be realistic about deadlines and hold your team to them.

Keep meetings short; 10-15 minutes is ideal. Have everyone literally stand up in the meeting to encourage each participant to be concise and efficient with their updates. Avoid cancelling or rescheduling meetings, even if only two people can attend.

If the team wants to share personal stories or chat with each other about their kids, ask them to arrive a few minutes early for this interaction or stay a few minutes afterwards.

Encourage honest conversations; even healthy conflicts are okay. Team members should be comfortable challenging each other, but no finger pointing, or blaming is allowed.

Time and place

The most beneficial examples involve teams working in the same location who can meet in the same room each day. However, if attendees are not physically present, phone or video conference is an option. Preferably, the daily meeting should begin soon after team members arrive and before their day gets started. For example, if the office opens at 8:30 AM, consider establishing an 8:45 AM meeting start time.

Agenda

Daily meetings do not follow a detailed agenda, but instead a consistent routine or matter plan. Once the meeting begins, the format is simple. Discuss and track activities that drive client value. This is not for internal initiatives or administrative projects. This is meant to deliver high level service to the client through precise execution of their matters.

Once the team has identified what is important to track, each attendee provides an update that includes what was accomplished the prior day, what they anticipate accomplishing that day, and any impediments to progress.

Visual management

Visual management is your friend. Develop a "production board" or method for easily displaying progress from day to day. Typically, whiteboards are used which allow you to modify the format before solidifying a standard layout for your team. Some organizations manage the board digitally through a software application designed for this purpose. Regardless, having a consistent visualization is the key point.

The visual routine helps the team establish expectations of what they are being asked to report, and of course, what gets measured gets done. Establish a routine for updating the production board (or software platform). In some organizations, team members are asked to update the board before the meeting begins as they find participants are more engaged when doing so. In others, the facilitator updates the board based on each participant's report out. Regardless, team members should be able to immediately identify positive or negative outcomes based on the board. As part of the post-meeting communication, the facilitator may take a picture of the board to distribute.

Problem solving and parking lots

Early implementation is going to expose many issues with your processes, especially if you lack standardization and do not have a continuous improvement program in your organization. This is not intended to be a problem-solving session. Most problems are too large to solve efficiently in this meeting. Because of this, you will need a "parking lot" for extended conversations that take on problem-solving.

A parking lot is a section on the board that allows the facilitator to note an issue that has been proposed which will be revisited outside of the meeting. Move the item to the parking lot and assign post-meeting action items to follow up.

As a side benefit, these meetings will reveal the maturity level of your organization's problem-solving skills. Over time, as you monitor problems and performance, you become more able to identify and focus on what is important and what is noise. The end goal is to show continuous improvement in the areas that have meaningful impact for the client and the organization.

Say nay to the naysayers

Implementation is not easy. Do not confuse this approach with typical meetings that currently consume your calendar. As you implement this, some team members will push back because it exposes weaknesses and forces a new level of productivity that the team is not accustomed to. If you are governed by the billable hour, there will be those who point out how costly the meeting is by having 10 people tied up for 15 minutes; however, just think how expensive it could be if those same 10 people each wasted half their day because of misunderstanding or lack of communication.

Understand the purpose

In the breakroom one day, a new paralegal team lead mentions casually to one of her peers. "Now that I'm in charge, we are going to stop having those team meetings. Just think about how much it costs the firm in billable hours. We should be doing more productive things with our time."

The previous team leader who had over 25 years of experience established the meetings years ago for a reason. It did not take long before mistakes were made from lack of direction and real time updates that typically came from those meetings. While well-intentioned, the new team lead did not fully appreciate the purpose, nor did she account for how to replace the communication.

Conclusion

After reading this chapter, hopefully you have reached the following conclusions:

- Daily management belongs in your organization;
- Implementation requires discipline, effort and lots of practice, but the benefits are significant; and
- Daily stand-up meetings are a great tool to enhance legal project management practices.

Remember, every day you have the same opportunity as your neighbor, so don't be like Jim.

Chapter 6:
Increasing profits and client value with legal project management practices

By Kathleen Thompson, formerly senior manager of client value and matter management at BakerHostetler

The premise of project management is "on-time delivery while being within budget and scope." Formal "project management" practices began with US military contractors in the 1950s; by the 1960s, the concept had spread into manufacturing. As the recession hit in the late 2000s, law firm clients began to focus on controlling spending and cost management. Demands for budgets and a stronger sense of financial accountability impacted all areas of a company. This shift in focus required law firms to quickly learn how to adapt and meet the demands of its clients.

Formal project management is a very detailed process, with many tools and techniques designed to manage projects and programs. However, many aspects of the project management framework are not applicable to legal work; an abbreviated version has therefore begun to form for the legal industry, called legal project management (LPM).

LPM is a discipline that captures the client's business goals, legal objectives, articulates assumptions, and identifies risks of a matter so a legal strategy can be developed. At its core, LPM is about asking and determining the answers to critical questions. The first step of the LPM process starts with a lawyer asking the client "why?" in order to fully understand the client's business and legal objectives. The next step is then for a lawyer to determine "what" needs to be done and the specifics of how, by whom and when the efforts will be executed to achieve the client's business strategy and legal goals. It is important to remember that even when there is a plan in place, the process of asking questions does not stop there, as LPM is an iterative process. It is critical for a lawyer to continue to ask questions so the plan and budget can be revised appropriately as circumstances change. Through discussions at the onset, a lawyer can define the "right" scope while strengthening the relationship with the client.

Since clients use project management, they expect their outside counsel to also speak the language and demonstrate that they have a consistent approach to managing their clients' legal matters. Many lawyers are already "doing" certain elements of LPM and know LPM is integral to developing the strategy for the matter. The LPM methodology enables a lawyer to understand the client's environment, culture, risk appetite, and financial health; LPM tools provide templates to document and communicate a plan, performance, status, and changes to the client. The tools demonstrate to the client that a lawyer is more than outside counsel: if a lawyer uses LPM, they are showing the client they are a "true partner," with a plan and process to execute a legal solution.

Traditionally, most law firms believe offering an alternative fee arrangement is LPM; however, as many eventually learn, strategic pricing is not LPM. Before developing an LPM program it is critical to ensure the firm leadership understands the difference: Strategic pricing is a sales technique and LPM is a value-add practice. LPM, not a pricing arrangement, creates value for a firm by increasing profits and generating value for the client through communication from plan to result.

Unfortunately, many lawyers feel LPM is additional administrative work. This is a myth. Leveraging LPM actually streamlines and documents what the lawyer and client have discussed. By documenting the agreed scope of legal work and communicating progress, LPM improves client communication and satisfaction. LPM can help reduce surprises in terms of effort and cost for both the law firm and client.

So, if the client is demanding project management, how can a law firm make sure their lawyers have a LPM process and believe in it enough to use the program and tools?

This chapter is highlights three recommendations to consider when developing a LPM program:

1. Hire a person who is not a lawyer from the client side;
2. Know the environment and current metrics in the firm; and
3. Diversify the initial roll-out.

The recommendations outlined can be leveraged independently, but applying all three to an LPM program concurrently will maximize the adoption speed firm-wide with the lawyers, and will demonstrate to the client that the law firm can manage the matters.

Leverage a different background

Bringing in a person from the client side is a unique approach that provides a law firm with a powerful "differentiator" from other firms. Everyone loves having access to information, especially when it increases profits. By bringing in someone who was in a finance role, they can share the "secrets" of the finance, procurement and operation leaders' environment and priorities. These stakeholders within the client – who are not lawyers -typically have substantial influence on outside counsel selection, guidelines and payments.

A professional with a financial and project management background from the client side who can share insights and real-life examples, becomes an invaluable resource to the lawyers. A lawyer who knows how these stakeholders think and whounderstands what is important to these clients can be remarkably instrumental in the success and growth of their firm. It is the finance person on the client's side who withholds payment of invoices to manage corporate cash flow and decline payments submitted substantially past the work date. It is the procurement person on the client's side who typically sets discounts, volume rebates and guidelines. Notably, it is the business leaders who set the strategy for future periods on legal spending – not the in-house counsel. When a firm is not selected for legal work, it is partially because the client was not satisfied with the firm's response regarding the billing process, matter management or communication plan.

In a former financial role at a manufacturing company, I was the financial lead for the global integration program on a $450 million transaction. Although the general counsel for the transaction was the legal point of contact for the outside counsel firms, they were not the lead on other aspects of the matter. The general counsel was certainly kept informed and consulted, but it was the operational leads and I who demanded credits on late invoices or invoices non-compliant with guidelines. Regularly I was the person within the company who advised the general counsel when a law firm needed to be replaced due to pricing or lack of communication regarding budget and/or status updates.

Clients want a partnership and proof that external counsel can manage legal matters while staying within the budget. A client will be more comfortable engaging with lawyers who can speak their language. Even if a firm is billing the client hourly, clients still want to know the answers to the following questions:

- How much it the effort going to cost?
- How long is it going to take?
- What is involved?
- Who should and will be involved?
- What are key events and deciding factors?

LPM is the process to ensure the questions are being asked, in order to properly scope and execute the legal work. It is a professional from the client's side, however, that can help ensure communiation about information and requirements the client needs to characterize the legal work as successful. Having a professional who can share these insights is a powerful strategy but should not be the only strategy.

Know the culture and key information

When developing an LPM program it is critical to make sure the law firm's culture and goals are documented and then incorporated into the design and roll-out. If the LPM program does not consider the firm's culture and what is important to the firm's leadership, the program will most likely be unsuccessful. However, if the LPM program is focused on improving an individual lawyer's metrics, the program should gain momentum, enthusiasm and buy-in from the lawyers.

Ensuring the firm metrics are highlighted in reports that the LPM function delivers to lawyers immediately allows a lawyer to understand the impact of the LPM program. Besides understanding what is currently being measured, the LPM program should also investigate what information is not being captured but could impact profitability and client satisfaction. Once the unknowns are identified, there is an opportunity to leverage the system and measure those metrics. Regardless, reporting through the LPM program should assist the lawyer in driving changes to profitability and impact client value.

An example of relevant information is an effort worked by a lawyer but not billed to the client. Legal work recorded to a matter but not billed or known will most likely will be written off in a future period. Without a performance report on the matter, the lead lawyer typically has no systematic way of knowing hours worked but not billed. If the lawyer does not have a way to know what has yet to be billed in a timely manner, the lawyer might lose out on billable revenue.

Similarly, I convinced a lawyer to use task codes on a matter. Time entries were already being entered by the lawyers working on the engagement, so they simply had to select a task code related to work they were recording to the engagement. This allowed the lead lawyer to discover early on that a team member was working inefficiently on a specific task and realized many of the hours would have to be written off. The lead lawyer addressed the inefficiencies of the team member and avoided future write-offs. The task codes also provided a summary of the work by task and key milestone. The lawyer leveraged this information to explain work efforts to the client; in turn, this allowed the client to understand the legal work more clearly and was therefore willing to accepted a revised budget and pay invoices without issue.

In rolling out the program, a key partner in leadership was quoted saying: "Performance reports come in very handy when we get client or insurer inquiries about how we are doing against budgets, and they have the added effect of giving us internal information that we can use to predict future budgets and track profitability." By leveraging LPM, through the use of task codes and performance reports, the practice matters in this group improved by over six percentage points in seven months.

Moreover, highlighting opportunities to increase profitability and/or billings will be well received by the lawyers, but it is critical to remember to keep metrics and reports simple. A lawyers' focus is legal work and knowledge, not budget and performance reports. As long as a lawyer does not have to spend time learning how to read a report, they will use the report information and see the tangible benefits.

When the lawyers make more money, they are happy; when they score high marks, they are happy; and when the new tools show value to the client, the lawyers are thrilled and will be more on inclined to leverage LPM.

Listen, learn, apply and adjust

Even using the inside track of insights from a client's a financial professional, and leveraging a firm's metrics for quick hits, there is a third recommendation an LPM program should encompass for a successful enterprise wide roll-out. Once a program has been developed, the initial roll-out needs to cover as much of the firm's environment as possible. Ensuring that all practice groups and a majority of the geographic locations are represented will allow a program to capture any unique attributes needing to be incorporated into the LPM program.

While the LPM methodology can be applied as a standardized concept to most law firms without significant adjustments, the tools need to be customized for the individual law firm. Factors that can contribute to the tool customization are but not limited to: the firm's goals and culture; size of firm; practice areas; and systems for time entry and financials. For example, a firm focused solely on employment law might leverage different tools than a firm involved in transactions or tax planning. A LPM program does not create nor attempt to implement aspects that will not benefit the lawyers in the firm nor its clients.

When the initial group (a.k.a. "pilot group") of lawyers represent the various practice areas and are geographically diverse, it will be easier to understand the tools needed and initate a smoother roll-out of the program across the entire firm. A well balanced "pilot" group should be ideally represented by the following:

- 40–50 percent of firms' offices; and
- 100 percent of the core practice groups.

The implementation trend is to roll out a program by office or practice group. Rolling out by office or practice group can be successful, but usually the program will not be adopted by the entire firm. A specific practice group might not feel they need to improve or want to change; a geographic region or office might say they know their clients and don't have time to adopt a new process. When the pilot group represents the majority of the firm, lawyers believe it is the focus of the firm and do not want to be excluded. Another benefit of a cross-functional team is it brings insight and encourages networking among the lawyers typically limited to their own area of practice. The cross-functional group approach allows the lawyers to be part of a "intrapreneur group", which is viewed as an elite opportunity.

A diverse pilot group creates a challenge for the LPM program management, as having various practice groups and broad demographics adds a layer of complexity. A solution is to create a case study to be used as a reference guide while the LPM methodology and tools are discussed. The benefit of the case study is that it allows the lawyers to "see" how LPM can drive higher profits, avoid write-offs, and improve client value. The case study should be substantial and, if possible, cover all practice groups of the firm and LPM tools developed.

The firm retained a consultant with whom I partnered to write a case study for an LPM training program that focused on implementation not just theory. Dividing the effort into three phases ensures a case study incorporates the LPM methodology, process stages, and tools. The three phases are:

1. Write the case study with one practice group covering all of the LPM process stages to create a foundation;
2. Next, layer in additional practice groups to ensure the case will be relevant to all lawyers in the firm and will show how a legal matter can require multiple practice groups to be involved with a single client legal situation; and
3. Finally, to have the biggest impact on the lawyers, incorporate the LPM tools into the case study to provide a "live" example on how the tools work and assisting the lawyers to understand the LPM. Our LPM consultant had practiced law for many years and she helped us meet this challenge.

Diversifying the pilot group attendees and materials can be the key to a successful and differentiating LPM program and implementation.

Reflect and revise

All learnings are valuable and should be analyzed to determine if an action should be taken to improve the LPM program. Common takeaways after a pilot can be (but are not limited to):

- 20–25 percent of the lawyer population will not buy-into the LPM concept and tools;
- 30–40 percent of the lawyer population will think they are using the program but are not or will only use one or two aspects; and
- 40–60 percent of tools will need to be adjusted based on pilot group discussions.

There is not one recipe to develop or improve an LPM program. What works for one firm might not work for another, but these recommendations provide the flexibility to adjust for the environment. The intent is that these recommended approaches prove insightful and thought-provoking.

LPM is like a kitchen. Every bowl or utensil is not used for every meal. The dishes and utensils used are appropriate for what is being made, how much time there is to prepare, and who is coming over for dinner. Every meal will have different requirements, and even the same meal will vary in its preparation each time it is made. Like cooking, adaptability and flexibility are the secrets to a successful LPM program.

Chapter 7:
Close collaboration drives successful outcomes

By Kevin Bielawski and Lann Wasson, director and associate director of legal project management at Husch Blackwell

When a large, nationally recognized retirement community assessed the cost of its legal services in 2015, its leadership concluded that the company needed to achieve greater predictability, transparency and value for the dollar in its legal spend. With a mission to provide the best possible care and service to its own residents, the company sought a different approach than paying numerous law firms by the hour to focus on distinct legal needs. The company collaborated with Husch Blackwell to develop a solution that would source all the company's legal work under an alternative pricing model.

Initially a series of fixed fee options with carve-outs for larger projects was discussed, but this idea was dropped because the company's leadership decided the proposal had too many caveats and stipulations. The company wanted a comprehensive arrangement that shared risk and aligned incentives to control costs and increase value. To facilitate development of such a proposal, the company's leadership team agreed to share with the firm the company's legal spend by practice area from the last three years. After consulting with the company's leadership about the risk profile derived from the data, Husch Blackwell proposed a comprehensive three-year, fixed fee arrangement with a collar above and below the fee. Work performed above the collar would be charged at a very substantial discount of the standard rates, while work below the collar would be partially credited back.

To successfully share risk and align incentives, the implementation of legal project management (LPM) with a client portal became an essential part of the arrangement for both the company and the firm. Husch Blackwell's project management program emphasizes strong communication protocols and follows a set of standards throughout the five phases of the matter life cycle (scoping, planning, managing, monitoring and post-project review), but also allows for customization to fit the needs of each client.

For this engagement, the shared objectives of the LPM program were:

- Legal expense control and predictability;
- Transparency in financial reporting;
- Efficient administration of new projects, from intake to invoicing;
- Shared understanding of project scope and budgets among all stakeholders; and
- Development of value-based metrics.

To fulfill these objectives, the firm – in collaboration with the company's leadership – designed a framework to align teams, projects, budgets, financial reporting and measurements of success with those of the company.

Team meetings

To facilitate communication, the firm established a client service team (CST) consisting of the relationship partner, lead attorneys servicing the distinct practice areas and non-attorney project management and finance professionals. The CST meets monthly to review the status of current projects and address issues. The budget is reviewed, and future demand is forecast. The non-attorney professionals train the attorneys on project management techniques and introduce practical ways to develop shared expectations around scoping and budgeting.

On the client side, the firm's project management and finance professionals plan quarterly joint meetings with the company's chief executives, business directors and the firm's CST. The joint meetings are used to review the goals and progress, current activity and projected legal spend, and drivers of current and future projects. Feedback is elicited on improvements to the portal, and next steps are suggested. After each quarterly joint meeting, a project management professional summarizes the discussion and describes future action items, responsibilities, and the timetable for the implementation of additional best practices.

Project alignment

One of the keys to reducing the administrative burden on both sides was to develop a matter structure that aligned with the company's general ledger, so that projects could be coded and tracked efficiently. To provide simplicity for those submitting projects on the business side and the firm lawyers coding their time, the number of matters was intentionally limited. The company's general ledger had three primary components that the firm added as attributes to the matters in its accounting system.

An automated intake workflow was developed that allowed the company's director of compliance and other business directors to submit projects to Husch Blackwell lawyers through the portal. The workflow included embedded logic so that projects were coded accurately and routed to the appropriate firm team members. The format also provided a way for the company to state the urgency and desired work product (email, memo, call, etc.). The firm attorneys received an email alert when a new project was submitted and accepted the project through the portal. Both sides could contribute notes during the submission and acceptance process to provide additional context. This approach also allowed the company to review project status in real time and see which legal professional was performing the work.

Financial reporting

In addition to the forecasts shared during internal CST meetings and quarterly joint meetings, the client portal offers a variety of online reports aligned with the company's fiscal year and updated nightly. The company's directors of finance and compliance, chief finance officer and firm lawyers can view the legal spend by matter and by each of the three components of the business' general ledger. The financial information was originally summarized in tabular and visual formats. Over time, these reports were augmented to provide additional detail and month-to-month views of legal spend to better align with the company's accounting processes. In fact, the company's director of finance exports the data from Husch Blackwell's portal in a custom format and loads it directly into the company's accounting system.

In the second year of the program, the company implemented budget accountability at the department level for operational projects. The ability to view spend by department and drill into the projects that contributed to that spend allows the company's business directors and the firm lawyers working on their projects up-to-date information on budget status. Having this information on hand aids both sides when clarifying expectations about the cost of a new project.

At a more administrative level, the portal also provides the kind of transparency to remedy errors in project assignment and coding of time. Initially, the number of transfers and reversals were on the high side as all participants became acclimatized to the new matter structure. But over time, the number of accounting changes fell sharply, saving time for both the firm and the company, in addition to painting a more accurate picture of the drivers of legal spend.

Measurements of success

Since an alternative fee arrangement and LPM program were new to the company, both sides recognized that it would take at least three years to more accurately forecast the volume of work expected and corresponding budget amounts. Compounding this issue was the volume of claims in inventory at the start of the arrangement, and the perception that the cycle time of claims was accelerating.

In this context, one of the primary objectives was to reduce the average monthly spend. Now in the middle of the engagement's second year, the efforts on both sides to contain costs and provide transparency have already produced a positive outcome. Average monthly legal spend has dropped by 16 percent year over year. With the continued focus on the client's objectives and the introduction of scoping and budgeting earlier this year, both sides continue to expect positive outcomes going forward.

Additionally, the company uses other value metrics to evaluate the success of the program. Some of those metrics include the speed of response time for matter initiation, the number of transfers and reversals to invoices, proactive projects that result in quantifiable savings, and improvements in the insurance loss ratio.

Success stories

A few examples illustrate the synergy and alignment which developed between the company's business team and firm lawyers. In one CST meeting, the relationship partner noted that when clients ask for guidance on an issue, they often are not requesting a comprehensive memo, but a "bullet point" version which allows the client to understand the salient points and make a sound business decision. Lawyers often perceive that any approach other than the "turn over every rock" method as less than adequate. While providing a "CliffsNote" version never means sacrificing quality, it does require lawyers to pay more attention to the business situation. When the topic was raised at the next quarterly joint meeting, the company's business directors responded that this was exactly the approach they desired. As the conversation unfolded, the CEO mentioned how refreshing it was to have a legal team be so conscious of the cost involved in performing the work.

During another CST meeting, there was a conversation about a training session performed by an expert from another firm office and the need to discuss how changes in scope must be aligned with budget expectations. In this case, the company's business directors began a back-and-forth with the presenter to include additional material in the deck and focus the topic on specific questions related to the company. Since the time involved in revising the deck was charged as legal fees, the final cost of training exceeded expectations. During the next quarterly joint meeting, a company business director asked how the teams could work together to do better next time. The discussion that followed addressed the root cause of the issue, but also explored other ways of lowering the cost, such as video-conferencing or even video training through the company's learning management system. These discussions were so productive that the company's director of compliance invited the firm's lawyers and project management professionals to participate in the company's internal lessons learned meetings.

Finally, at the start of the second fiscal year, the firm's project management professionals introduced the practice of scoping and budgeting to the CST. The project management professionals shared a template for use with the company and walked the firm's lawyers through real-world examples from previous projects. After this session, more of the lawyers started asking the company's business directors whether they should jointly develop scoping statements for new matters and confirm budget expectations.

In a subsequent training session on scoping and budgeting by the firm's project management professionals with the company's business directors, the CEO interrupted the program to highlight that the scoping exercise might actually lead to the firm doing less work. The example he gave was a library of construction contracts, developed by one of the firm lawyers, for the business directors to use in typical contract scenarios. Instead of the firm producing every contract – even standard ones – at a cost, the company could take on some of the contracting, using language already vetted by the firm.

In the next quarterly joint meeting, the CFO continued this theme when he recounted how the scoping process allowed one of the firm's attorneys to ask whether the CFO wanted to attend a city planning meeting in his place. Usually a law firm would attend all of the meetings and charge the client accordingly, but since a firm lawyer didn't need to be at this meeting, there was an opportunity to reduce the cost of the project. The CFO was more than happy to attend and was pleasantly surprised at the attention paid to delivering the overall service at the best value.

These examples underscore the importance of ongoing dialogue around scoping and budgeting, so that there is optimal utilization of a lawyer's skills and time on a project. Involving project management and finance professionals directly with the client's business team also furthered the goals of the engagement and reduced the firm's attorney administrative time, allowing the firm attorneys to focus on the relationship and legal work.

Legal project management is often implemented within a law firm as a means for lawyers to deliver greater value to their clients. However, the practical activities of project management can be even more effective when clients and law firms jointly and actively participate in the process. In this case study, the benefits of close collaboration between Husch Blackwell and its client are evident in the alignment of teams, projects, financial reporting, and measurements of success. The hard metrics of substantially lowering average legal spend per month, the new value metrics and the success stories indicate that LPM is an excellent approach not only to contain cost, but also to deliver exceptional client service.

Chapter 8: Legal service delivery innovation – a case study in mitigating six law firm biases

By Samuel Davenport and Brian Fanning, director of legal business solutions and director of practice economics at Davis Wright Tremaine

Legal project management (LPM) is ready to evolve. At present its scholarship focuses on billable "matter management" – planning, executing, and reviewing the time, cost, scope, and quality of the legal *work product* in question[1] – but stops short of advising how that serviced work is best *delivered*, in order to fully satisfy the client.

In the last decade, LPM's structured approach to "matter management" has demonstrably increased efficiency and reduced the cost of lawyers and staff to produce excellent legal work. Now, in requests for proposals (RFPs) and outside counsel guidelines, clients often require legal project management capabilities. Yet as traditional LPM's adoption increases, it loses its force to attract clients away from competitor firms. Because they are largely fungible, law firms can lay claim to very few competitive differentiators: namely, legal work and service delivery.[2] Traditional "matter management" LPM provides tools to ensure the legal work stays excellent, but it lacks tools to ensure the service delivery addresses client needs in a way that at least satisfies, and, ideally, delights.[3] Without a way to innovate current service delivery, law firms are less able to meet what ought to be the second twin aim of any professional services firm: delighting the client (see Figure 1 overleaf).

Service delivery is critical to delighting today's clients

Legal service delivery is the means and method by which legal work product is transmitted to the client. Traditionally, legal work is delivered as *outcomes* (e.g., settlement, trial wins, successful mergers), *work product* (e.g., pleadings, motions, contracts), and *advice* (e.g., face-to-face counsel, internal memos, guidance by telephone). Law firms spend enormous effort on making legal work excellent. They set the acceptance criteria as to whether the counsel given is correct and prudent;[4] most often this

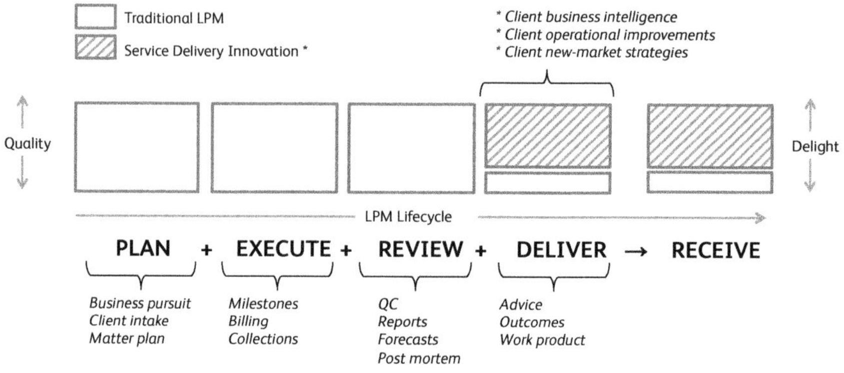

Figure 1: Service delivery innovation attached to traditional "matter management" LPM framework

acceptance criteria is exclusively controlled by the fee earner, with little in the way of client input. Unfortunately, even the value of excellent legal work can be diminished when the client is given no explicit way to better capitalize on or contextualize that work.

As clients focus on the value they receive from law firms in terms of both *work* and *delivery*, they also grow the need to understand the legal work they are buying in the context of their specific business needs. Responsive law firms generate service delivery innovations to keep pace with the client's new legal requests and its changing business needs. Those innovations come in three varieties: changes to people (e.g., partnering with a lower cost alternative legal services provider to execute less skill-intensive or commodified work); changes to processes (e.g., designing a contract management lifecycle with custom escalation paths from business owners to in-house legal subject matter experts to multiple outside counsel); or changes to tools (e.g., building a secure litigation matter tracking dashboard built on a collaboration platform).[5]

Innovations in how legal work is delivered help ensure that excellent, inscrutable work product retains its value even when it passes from the insulated corridors of the law firm to the raw reality of the business world.

Service delivery innovation can be a force multiplier for value by increasing the amount and quality of the client's:

- **Business intelligence**. The information about how the client uses the legal services is sometimes as valuable as the actual service. A law firm, by capturing metadata from a client's large body of procurement contracts, can create an interactive visual analysis so the client can see the range of concessions and outcomes in the most negotiated provisions of a given class of contract and make better policy about when it should contest or accept terms;

- **Legal operations**. In instances where in-house law departments are burdened with areas of high volume, low value work – such as spurious third-party subpoenas – a law firm can design a process, partner an expert team, and build a tool, all to rapidly triage subpoenas that ought to receive immediate attention and support from those that can stand to be worked in the order received; and
- **New-market strategies**. Law firms can help a client extend its reach to previously unknown markets and customers. In introducing a legal service provider (LSP) previously unknown to the client, a law firm can serve a matchmaking role and extend the client's strategic reach to new markets with new services contracted by the LSP under the client's own banner.

These innovations require significant investment of capital, time, and people by the law firm. Using a discrete department for designing, prioritizing, and launching such innovations, the law firm can dependably deploy new service delivery models targeted to provide excellent work product (for the client's legal needs) by way of excellent service delivery (for its business needs). However, while the value to the client is immediately apparent, law firms tend to underinvest in service delivery innovation. Largely owing to a series of six cultural biases, the typical law firm culture is anathema to service delivery innovation efforts.

Six biases make law firms especially hard soil in which to grow innovation

While, yes, "change is hard, period,"[6] the difficulties of changing the culture in a law firm are especially pronounced. Specifically, biases shared by most law firms make rebuffing innovation – especially large-scale change – a virtual certainty. Law firms share biases in relation to *training*, *form*, *incentive*, *mindset*, *investment*, and *risk* that are all inhospitable to innovation.

1. Training

Law, like medicine, is a business of hyper-specialization. Most lawyers in large law firms have specialized by their second year of practice and stick with that specialty sometimes for their entire career. Because law demands mastery of precedent and minutiae in few subject areas, lawyers who spend that considerable energy researching specialized information do not equally indulge in the diffuse, decentralized, cross-discipline thinking necessary to apply an advancement in one area to an advancement in a completely different area (a process central to innovation). Broad autonomy accorded to each practice group compounds the siloing of talent and increases the need for de-specialization even further if a law firm wants to standardize innovative thinking.

2. Form

Unlike C-corporations or LLCs, the structure of general and limited liability partnerships precludes unilateral decision making. At Davis Wright Tremaine, when we meet with management consultants to discuss innovation initiatives, most have rarely worked with a law firm. Inevitably, at some point they hear about so many stakeholders of the project and ask: "Just who exactly is the business owner making the buying decision?" In answering, law firms must detail a complex diagram of different business owners located in multiple practice areas, with no single decision maker immediately apparent.[7]

The practical result is that the bigger and more expensive the initiative, the more likely the effort will be managed by (and likely die in) committee. These committees are ad-hoc and not necessarily trained in management or finance, and often the lease/buy/build decisions are made on gut and instinct alone.

3. Incentive

The billable hour is popularly decried as inefficient,[8] obsolete,[9] and already dead.[10] Yet, it remains a reality of law firm life and the primary way in which legal services are valued.[11] Even if clients continue to demand more AFAs, law firms have built fee-earner performance review, partner candidate tracking, and attorney and partner compensation all around billable hour requirements. At most law firms, any lawyer not maximally utilized is taking dollars out of the pockets of partners. When pro bono hour requirements and administrative tasks are added to the billable requirements, the hours needed to properly innovate – design, test, iterate, redesign, test, iterate – become nearly impossible to find.

4. Mindset

Lawyers are a unique breed not just by training: those who join and thrive at a law firm share several defining characteristics. On balance, they are change averse and tend to be more autonomous, more skeptical, more urgent, less sociable, and less resilient than a member of the general population.[12] In contrast, creating a culture of innovation requires process standardization, cross-functional collaboration, taking calculated risks, and curiosity to push established boundaries.[13]

5. Investment

Law firms tend to prefer conservative, proven, and uncontroversial investments because they run on capital contributions from their many equity partners. Whereas in a corporation a senior VP may have compensation incentives that create a personal interest in reducing expenses that decrease the total profits of the company, every equity partner in a law firm may want to be consulted (at the very least) in expense decisions, since the operating capital is in a very real sense their own money. Given the high number of equity partners, and the depth of their interest, large-scale capital investments must be thoroughly vetted and highly popular to pass muster. Innovation investments, often with unknowable outcomes, are rarely conservative investment plays.

6. Risk

Law firms, which give consumers little in the way of comparators and which disproportionately win work on the strength of reputation, avoid risk. Indeed, managing client risk and reducing client stress are arguably the most important services law firms provide. Although much has been made of applying lean startup business practice to law firms, the two businesses differ in at least one compelling way. A startup can tolerate substantial failed attempts at service, provided it gets at least one right. A company that launches 10 failed products but then launches an indispensable 11th can be a unicorn with a billion-dollar valuation. Conversely, a law firm that loses 10 sizable matters while winning a notable 11th should only hope to be wound down and shuttered. Even properly managed innovation projects have a high probability of failure,[14] and the chance of highly publicized failures are nonstarters when it comes to persuading a firm to launch such a project.

Case study: legal services delivery innovation at Davis Wright Tremaine (DWT De Novo)

In early 2013, the leadership at Davis Wright Tremaine – a mid-sized AMLAW 100 firm with around 500 lawyers – championed an innovation initiative to improve legal services delivery and pricing, and to inculcate a culture of innovation. The firm named a chief innovation partner (CIP) responsible for soliciting new ideas for better process improvement and service delivery from lawyers and staff. As the list of ideas grew, so did the resources needed to vet, plan, and produce working prototypes of those ideas. In late 2013, the firm designated a seven-member innovation team made up of the CIP, a project manager, an IT liaison, and analysts in business development, marketing, quality control, finance, and operations.

As members of a "volunteer army," these team members played roles on the innovation team in addition to their primary day jobs. Early projects with interminable timelines made it plain that, to get the necessary traction to execute and implement the collected ideas, the firm needed to dedicate full-time headcount to the team. The team was trimmed down to the CIP, project managers, and a business development analyst. It was named "DWT De Novo," but retained a much larger volunteer army (those closely affiliated and doing DWT De Novo work).

In both 2015 and 2016, new service delivery solutions that DWT De Novo built helped the law firm win the International Legal Technologists Association (ILTA) Innovative Firm of the Year Award. In 2016, similar solutions helped DWT win the *Financial Times*' Innovative Lawyers Awards North America's US Standout for "Redesigning the service & delivery model." In 2017, DWT won Top Firm in that same category and was included in the FT's list of 25 most innovative law firms overall.[15] In 2018, just prior to this book going to press, it was nominated as a finalist for a Legal Services Innovation Award from *The American Lawyer.*

These accomplishments were happy by-products of the firm's commitment to innovation in its 2012 strategic plan. To accomplish any degree of success, the firm had to overcome each of the six biases of law firms, mentioned above.

1. Training

Attorneys at law firms specialize, and each of these specialists is a potential source of better service delivery for their client. Because the DWT De Novo team is just one small department (outnumbered by a pool of energetic partner sponsors), it employs generalists. To assist a partner in exploring and designing a new idea, and to do so in a way that safeguards prudence and pragmatism, requires skill sets not yet commonly found in most law firms. To span these gaps, DWT De Novo commissioned the role of Legal Solution Architect (LSA).[16]

An LSA has expertise in three specific domains. First, an LSA understands and employs *business analysis* tools to better understand: the features of a particular idea, how the idea is different than others proposed, how its features match current law firm resources, and its potential upside. These tools include requirement gathering techniques, feature prioritization, stakeholder management, and go-to-market strategies. Second, to compensate for the partner sponsor's busy schedule, the LSA has *project accountability* for an idea's design, implementation, and maintenance. LSAs have training in a variety of project management and change management methods such as waterfall, agile, lean, and six sigma. Finally, LSAs build expertise in the *innovation thought leadership* of the firm by cataloguing and reporting on wins, failures, and lessons learned on projects in a bid for continuous improvement of the DWT De Novo department.

This expertise and training allows LSAs to manage the development of a partner sponsor's idea – a legal business solution – in relation to: the desire and cost to the client and/or firm; the internal architecture and capability of existing people, process, and tools; and the external offering of business partners or third-party providers.

2. Form

Because law firms lack a strong ability to make quick, unilateral decisions, the DWT De Novo group launches many small initiatives at one time, each with its own partner sponsor and project manager. Whereas a corporation with a hierarchical structure might become confused and overwhelmed by so many projects being undertaken without central control or notice, a law firm is already used to supporting a host of simultaneous decentralized programs, provided that some standard process keeps every project as profitable as possible.

In DWT De Novo, the innovation team is trained to listen to an initial partner sponsor's idea and then ask questions[17] to increase the positive *impact* on the firm (in terms of revenue or reputation) and decrease the *effort* necessary to bring the idea to life. The DWT De Novo team uses a paper template called a Solution Idea Canvas to map a partner's idea.

The Canvas prompts a structured conversation in four parts. First, a back and forth with the partner about the history of the idea and its uniqueness to the market. Second, the LSA reviews the business use case and asks a battery of questions to quantify the effort to make the idea real versus the impact a successful project will have on the firm. Third, the LSA reviews current available and applicable people, process, and tool resources with the partner sponsor. Finally, the LSA guides the partner sponsor through an exercise designed to get value faster, get bigger impact, and broaden the application of the project.

Each idea is catalogued, tracked, and prioritized, with top priority going to the most energetic partner sponsor (energy usually created by having the largest potential revenue upside). One of the DWT De Novo's earliest lessons learned was that the power to prioritize innovation projects for the firm should not rest with the innovation team (DWT De Novo), because proper prioritization requires analyzing all the collected ideas against all the potential practice area growth, the costs and benefits of each idea, and then current technical, infrastructural, and personnel capabilities and resources of the firm as a whole. That kind of holistic analysis is better suited for a cross-functional committee comprising executive-level fee earners and staff. In absence of such a committee, however, individual partners – aided by members of the innovation team – prove more than capable of lobbying for firm resources for their individual projects, and this natural competition for limited resources produces a healthy model for which projects should be augmented, implemented, or abandoned.

3. Incentive

Although some law firms have found success creating innovation teams of hybrid fee-earners, DWT De Novo intentionally builds its core team of legal solution architects (LSAs) with non-practicing lawyers and business consultants. Believing its practitioners have the ideas, if not the time nor technical skills, to innovate service delivery, it developed a core innovation team solely dedicated to cultivating and executing the best ideas of DWT practitioners. This team is wholly staff-side and has no billable hour requirements, allowing it to move quickly when necessary, and eliminating any bias that might occur if the core team members were earning fees for individual practice groups.

4. Mindset

Given attorneys' predilection to be more autonomous, skeptical, and urgent, and less sociable and resilient than average, a law firm's innovation group should build its staff to compensate for these characteristics, while sharing enough of them to encourage fluid interaction. In practice for DWT De Novo, this means building a role that can be credible enough to start a trusting relationship, while deferential enough to keep the partner sponsor squarely in the role of "solution champion". The majority of DWT De Novo LSAs are non-practicing attorneys, and those who aren't have deeper experience in business analysis. While there doesn't appear to be any concrete skill learned in law school or practice that makes an LSA more apt and able to help bring a partner sponsor's idea into reality, for whatever reason the process encounters less friction when the LSA has or is actively earning a professional school credential.

Beyond credibility and deference, the innovation group also needs to de-silo information (about the project, the practice, the client, or the attorneys) so that it can make use of the firm's "volunteer army". This de-siloing is primarily accomplished by two types of periodic meetings. One type is a 15-minute "scrum-styled" project stand-up meeting[18] led by the LSA, which moves beyond project status to also solicit what competing priorities members of the team are working on. This meeting serves several important functions. It keeps the team informed of all challenges to the project; it provides a glimpse into the possibly unrelated tasks and challenges of all team members and presents opportunities for assistance and otherwise missed connections; and it generally familiarizes team members with each other. While a project may only last a couple of months, those months spent on a shared goal mean that members will be much more likely to reach out to each other in the future.

The second meeting type is one-on-one between LSAs and partners, executives, directors, managers, and any other employee who might have a perspective the LSA cannot currently see. These meetings are less regimented and center around capabilities and constraints.

At DWT, while the dedicated headcount for DWT De Novo has stayed small, its volunteer army ranks have dramatically ballooned. So many key members of successful service delivery innovation solutions sit in legal practice groups, finance, technology, administration, and marketing. This means that it is difficult to say where DWT De Novo begins and ends. We see this as an encouraging sign that idea by idea, the firm as a whole is beginning to encode innovation into its DNA.

5. Investment

Because the equity partners supply the capital for innovation projects, any law firm innovation group must be committed to being a good steward of the partners' money in as structured and transparent a way as possible. DWT De Novo accomplishes this in two ways. First, as discussed above, any innovation project is matched with a partner sponsor, who can make the case for capital expenditure to the firm's management committee. The prerequisite of a partner sponsor is critical to preventing DWT De Novo from making investment decisions – either in perception or in reality – on behalf of the firm. Second, every innovation project must pass through a series of decision gates wherein the LSA helps the partner sponsor explicitly explore alternatives to make the impact larger (e.g. by widening the market, increasing adoption, or broadening the use case) and to make the cost and effort smaller (e.g. by using existing tools, combining similar projects, or reducing the scope of work). For the life of the project, the LSA helps the partner sponsor finetune the best balance of impact and effort. Prescheduled milestone, effort, and impact reporting keeps the project from running off course or languishing without any progress.

When all projects are managed through this framework, equity partners' fears of waste are assuaged. Even if a project ultimately fails, the partners can trust that the project was executed as efficiently as possible and closed as soon as possible.

6. Risk

To protect strength of reputation accumulated over decades, law firms need to avoid public failures. However, as we have discussed, some tolerance to failure is necessary to properly encourage innovation. With the staff-side DWT De Novo, DWT is able to reconcile these opposing interests by creating day jobs for a team that prioritizes balancing effort and impact, making a "volunteer army" available for more subject-matter specific needs, and prioritizing the ideas of the most energetic partners (who usually receive that energy from critical client needs). The result is a pragmatic system that naturally diversifies its "innovation wagers" and prevents one or two initiatives from being overfunded or overengineered. Multiple projects competing for resources create a natural selection effect that dictates project failures are wound down early and quietly. Successful projects receive more resources commensurate with a new round of goals set by the partner sponsor, while the primary project management by an LSA means that no partners bear the stigma of any failed projects.

Law firm bias	Innovation obstacle	Obstacle mitigation
1. Training – specialized and isolated	Deters cross-disciplinary collaboration necessary for innovation by siloing practice groups and hyper-specializing fee earners.	Employing legal solution architects (LSAs) in a central position – full-time, staff-side generalists with expertise in business analysis, project accountability, and innovation thought leadership – to understand the firm's full range of resources and constraints and assist partner sponsors with project execution.
2. Form – limited partnership that precludes quick, unilateral decision making	Relegates the fate of innovation initiatives to large, ad-hoc committees that lack training in finance and management. Causes buy/build/lease decisions to be made on intuition alone.	Running many small projects at once, prioritized by analyzing: • all the collected ideas against all the potential practice area growth; • the costs and benefits of each idea; • current technical, infrastructural, and personnel capabilities and resources of the firm as a whole; and • the estimated upsides. By doing this, the innovation group can make decentralized, tactical decisions to keep priority projects on time and under budget.
3. Incentive – Billable hour production	Eliminates the availability of time of subject matter experts (fee-earners) needed to design, test, iterate, redesign, retest, and reiterate.	Staff-side LSAs with no billable hour requirements assist partner sponsors with the design and management innovation projects, using tools that allow partners to focus on the big-picture vision quickly and as efficiently as possible.

4. Mindset – Change-averse with low patience and resilience	Any innovation places lawyers in situations where change is a certainty, patience is needed to bear out results, and a string of setbacks is standard before a project succeeds.	Hiring LSAs who have business process credibility with the partner sponsor – but stay deferential in a way that encourages maximum partner participation – and de-silo project information by staying connected to all areas of the firm.
5. Investment – Conservative, proven, and uncontroversial	Demands consensus from a large group of equity partners with divergent and varied interests before launching innovation projects (which tend to be unproven investments).	Making it a primary responsibility of the innovation group to be a good steward of the partners' money by creating decision gates that force the weighing of cost versus return at various points in the project's lifecycle, and by requiring any project to have a partner sponsor who is responsible for the resources spent on the project.
6. Risk – Hypervigilance in protecting firm reputation from stigma of failure	Creates intolerance in the firm for projects with high, public risks of failure, because well-managed innovation projects often suffer a string of failures before finding success.	A dedicated service delivery innovation team that can run many small projects in a system that diversifies its innovation risk (and tolerates failure) and promotes those projects that promise the greatest impact for the least amount of effort, minimizing failures and keeping them private and disconnected from fee-earners.

Figure 2: Mitigating law firm biases to innovate service delivery

Differentiating legal service delivery requires mitigating the six biases inherent in law firm culture

As detailed above, traditional forms of LPM are becoming table stakes in the legal industry. Excellent legal work and effective matter management, while critical to meeting clients' expectations, will largely fail to delight clients who increasingly demand the delivery of legal services customized for their own legal *and* business needs. As entities, law firms express inherent biases that inhibit successful service delivery innovation. Figure 2, above, provides a systematic accounting of how Davis

Wright Tremaine's innovation group successfully mitigated those biases to pave the way for delivering client-focused service delivery.

References

1. Vermette, Madison, "The Life Cycle of a Matter," ILTA Blog, 05-23-2017 (Detailing the stages of LPM in matter management), https://www.iltanet.org/blogs/madison-vermette/2017/05/23/the-life-cycle-of-a-matter-lpm-pricing?ssopc=1.
2. Cohen, Mark, Forbes.com, "Differentiation in the New Legal Marketplace and Why it Matters," 01.02.2018, ("Law firm reliance on 'practice excellence,' pedigree, and reputation – without more – is no longer sufficient to be competitive or sustainable.").
3. See Fig. A.
4. Arguably, practitioners define the *value* of the legal work as the extent to which the work is correct and prudent, regardless of how the client receives the work or what the client does with it.
5. Ramakrishman, Sreekanth & Testani, Michael, "People, Process, Technology – The Three Elements for a Successful Organizational Transformation," IBM Center for Learning and Development, Presentation, 03.22.201.
6. Furlong, Jordan, "How to bring about change in law firms," https://www.law21.ca/2017/04/bring-change-law-firms/.
7. A law firm is a loose set of networked relationships, not a hierarchical command and control environment. This helps explain why so much of today's change management philosophies written for corporate hierarchies (John Kotter's 8 steps, ADKAR, and ProSci) face similar challenges regardless to which law firm they are applied.
8. Cassens Weiss, Debra, "Billable hour pricing is effectively dead because of budget caps, report says," *ABA Journal*, 01.12.2017.
9. McMullan Abramson, Leigh, "Is the Billable Hour Obsolete?", https://www.theatlantic.com/business/archive/2015/10/billable-hours/410611/.
10. Bradley, Ryan, "Why the Billable Hour is Dead (Or Should Be)," Forbes.com, https://www.forbes.com/sites/theyec/2017/05/26/why-the-billable-hour-is-dead-or-should-be/#57956aa55289.
11. Slaughter, Edward, Collier, S Christopher, and Arndt, Michael, "Cautious Optimism Over the Increasingly Prevalent Alternative Fee Arrangements," *Texas Lawyer*, 08.01.2018, (finding only 25% of all legal fees account for non-billable fee arrangements).
12. Richard, Larry, Managing Partner Forum, "Herding Cats: The Lawyer Personality Revealed," retrieved at http://www.managingpartnerforum.org/tasks/sites/mpf/assets/image/MPF%20-%20Herding%20Cats%20-%20Richard%20-%203-5-121.pdf (based on the Caliper Profile psychology test, lawyers on average score 20

percent more on autonomy, 40 percent more on skepticism, 21 percent more on urgency, 38 percent less on sociability, and 20 percent less on resilience than a member of the general public). More pointedly, "most lawyers hate change. They also love autonomy and resist rules and structure. They have little patience and want immediate results. They don't like risk and shun the unknown." https://www.americanbar.org/publications/law_practice_home/law_practice_archive/lpm_magazine_articles_v34_is7_pg28.html.

13. Metcalf, Maureen, "How To Create A Culture Of Innovation and Learning," Forbes.com, https://www.forbes.com/sites/forbescoachescouncil/2017/07/21/how-to-create-a-culture-of-innovation-and-learning/#4375fc4665f8.
14. Fisher, Anne, "Why most innovations are great big failures," Fortune.com, http://fortune.com/2014/10/07/innovation-failure/, (finding innovation projects tend to fail 90% of the time).
15. https://www.dwt.com/Davis-Wright-Tremaine-LLP-Named-Innovative-Law-Firm-of-The-Year-by-The-International-Legal-Technology-Association-09-02-2015/; https://www.dwt.com/Davis-Wright-Tremaine-Repeats-as-Innovative-Law-Firm-of-the-Year-08-31-2016/; https://www.dwt.com/Davis-Wright-Tremaine-Top-ranked-by-the-Financial-Times-Innovative-Lawyers-Awards-North-America-2016-12-09-2016/; https://www.dwt.com/Davis-Wright-Tremaine-Top-Ranked-by-the-Financial-Times-Innovative-Lawyers-Awards-North-America-12-13-2017/.
16. The LSA role is modeled after the Solution Architect role in the The Open Group Architecture Framework (TOGAF), which charts a high-level software development method consisting of: Business, Data, Applications, and Technology architectures. https://en.wikipedia.org/wiki/The_Open_Group_Architecture_Framework, https://www.cio.com/article/3251707/methodology-frameworks/what-is-togaf-an-enterprise-architecture-methodology-for-business.html.
17. Fisher, Fortune.com, Mark Payne, principal of innovation firm Fahrenheit 212, in explaining putting the "wow" before the "how" describes the necessity of rigorously questioning nascent ideas: "'Ideas are treated not as precious pearls to be polished, but as sparks born of friction' – because 'exposing fledgling innovation ideas to the tough love of tough questions … ensures those ideas can survive in the real world of real companies placing real bets with real money.'"
18. Daily scrum meetings are borrowed from the agile project management framework, which enables small teams to focus in several different areas at once, while managing and escalating all project obstacles. https://www.scrum.org/resources/what-is-a-daily-scrum. They are also discussed in detail in Chapter 5 of this book.

Chapter 9: How law departments use LPM to improve the corporate bottom line

By Aileen Leventon, principal of Edge International[1]

The discipline of project management provides a solid foundation for every activity conducted by a business. Legal project management (LPM) provides the discipline that enables law departments to define, demonstrate and deliver greater value to their organizations by balancing the scope of work, time, and resources allocated to legal work more efficiently. At its core, effective project management is about sound communication at critical points with the right stakeholders.[2] This ranges from colleagues to clients, external law firms to regulators.

Client needs and expectations for the delivery of valuable legal services have created pricing pressure on law firms. Law firms have seen LPM as a means of protecting margins and in responding to clients' inquiries about the firm's use of LPM in requests for proposals and ongoing outside counsel reviews. Many law firms have limited their use of LPM to the mechanics of budgeting, monitoring, and the broader goal of improving the economic results of a law firm. In-house counsel need to contribute to the corporate bottom line through their role as corporate employees while limiting the ever-expanding scope of client expectations about the role of in-house lawyers. In-house counsel can use LPM practices to assure the appropriate use of corporate resources to provide quality legal work through the use of scoping tools, checklists on legal issues, and other practice aids. Through this vantage point, it becomes evident that law firms use LPM too narrowly. By considering how lawyers serve a client in-house – either as a member of a legal department or a smaller internal organization of a company or government agency – it becomes evident that LPM is a robust framework for all lawyers.

The threshold: defining the role of the legal department

While each legal department and/or in-house lawyer may formulate its/

their role differently, the fundamental challenge of a lawyer in a business setting is to help clients achieve business goals, take advantage of opportunities, and protect against legal risk. Compliance with laws, regulations, and corporate policy are about both risk and reputation, which are integral to a company's business and culture.

Highly regarded and effective in-house lawyers are known for certain behaviors, in addition to their substantive legal expertise. They demonstrate skills that reflect the role of a lawyer as a trusted advisor, insofar as they:

- Understand all aspects of a client's business so legal services are calibrated to achieve the business definition of a successful result;
- Recognize that legal issues are one of many components in a client's business project or goal;
- Seek to add the most value by finding the lawyers with the appropriate level of experience who can support the business endeavor at the right time;
- Ensure that legal services and expenses and resources are aligned with business goals and strategies; and
- Participate in communication channels to ensure that the right level of communication occurs at the right time with the right stakeholders and professionals.

The general counsel and members of the legal department – lawyers, paralegals and operations professionals – are well-positioned to address these issues. They are able to integrate their understanding of the business context into everything they do, regardless of whether external counsel or other service providers are involved. In-house counsel manages the delivery of legal services to the client, while tactically managing a cost-effective action plan that achieves the client's business goals. LPM provides the tools and the methodology for meeting this challenge, while guarding against the impulse to work on the interesting legal issues at the expense of adding value to the company.

In-house counsel also faces the challenge of being called upon by clients to do work that is not within the remit of the legal department, and must diplomatically address this demand for allocation of resources. How many times has in-house counsel been asked to review a letter to a supplier so that the business person can claim he "ran it through legal" when the business deal is unsuccessful? And how can the lawyer push back by saying the request is out of scope of the role of the legal department since all that is involved is editing the grammar of a letter?

Representatives of the legal department also must translate the client perspective when retaining a law firm or other third party to participate in handling the matter. It is incumbent on the client to clearly articulate their view in order to guide the handling of the matter. How many discussions about the reasonableness of fees relate to the gap between outstanding legal work and the business needs of the client? And if the business needs are not well understood, to what extent is the inside counsel responsible for the lack of alignment? The law department must ensure that the entire legal team, including law firms, understand the importance of how the work is done, consistent with the corporate culture and needs.

Five questions to maintain focus

An LPM framework calls for legal team members to be able to answer five key questions at the launch of a matter and throughout its course in a manner appropriate to their roles. The questions should be reconsidered at critical junctures, particularly because of the likelihood of changes in circumstances. As new information emerges, assumptions made at the outset may not hold. Stakeholders within the company may be problematic because of disparate definitions of a successful outcome. Even in the absence of change, as time goes on and as the composition of the team evolves, it is important to confirm that all are headed toward the same goal in a consistent manner.

The five questions relate to both process (how the work is done) and substantive legal strategy and tactics.

1. WHY we are handling this matter for the business – why is it important to the company's strategy and operations?
2. WHAT legal strategy will accomplish the business goal and what legal work is out of scope?
3. WHEN and in what sequence must work be done, and what are the uncertainties and dependencies regarding timing?
4. HOW do we manage the work, given constraints and requirements such as budget, strategic importance, regulatory and reporting obligations, timing, and risk management protocols?

5. WHO is involved in the work and what is each person's role and responsibility?

The response should be tempered by the need to create a positive experience for the client in receiving advice and counsel from the legal team. Too often, lawyers – like other technical professionals – treat their expertise as the end in itself. Instead, it is the means to an end – namely, helping a client address a business issue or opportunity. The service delivery model should reflect empathy for the client and an understanding of his or her perspective.

The answers to these questions have consequences – positive, negative and neutral – for resource allocation, work plans, scope of work, stakeholders, roles and responsibilities, teamwork, training, communications throughout the project, status reporting, and client satisfaction. The systematic analysis of these issues addresses the operational challenges of the legal department by reducing non-value added (or wasted) time, minimizing surprising outcomes and costs, managing overall costs and spending, and controlling time to completion more precisely.

Four stages of a matter

LPM applies the business discipline of project management across four stages through which all matters flow:

1. Intake;
2. Planning;
3. Execution; and
4. Review.

This framework, developed by a 2017 Corporate Legal Operations Consortium (CLOC) group of experts,[4] is illustrated in Figure 1. It updates work done by the Association of Corporate Counsel in 2012, in its legal project management primer.[5]

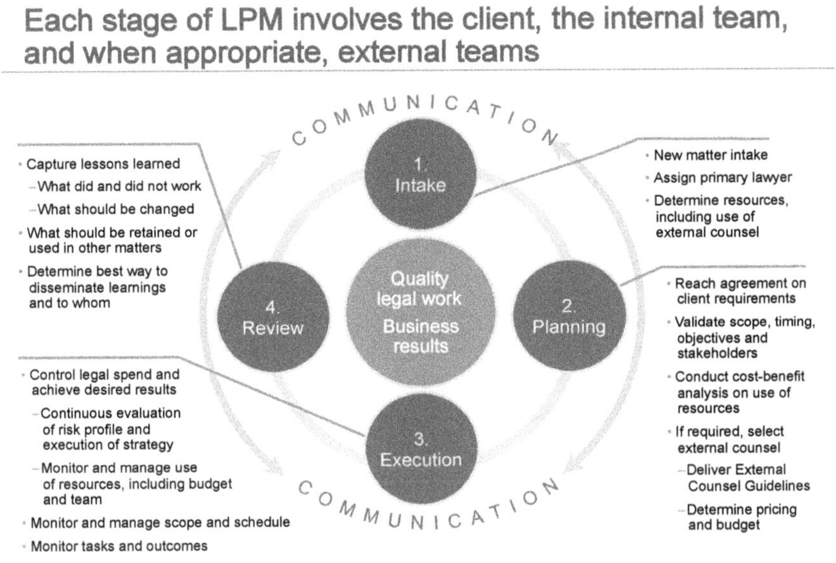

Figure 1: The legal project management framework. Source: https://cloc.org/industry-guidelines – CLOC Legal Project Management (LPM) for Legal Teams; The Business Case and Action Plan for Legal Departments.

Intake

Intake occurs when the legal department becomes involved – after confirming the validity of the request as appropriate. Many in-house counsel are faced with client requests for support that are inappropriate, since legal risks do not meet a threshold or there are no real legal issues involved. As much as the lawyer wants to be a valued partner to the business team, the intake phase is the point at which the lawyer may have to diplomatically push back and manage the demand for services. Scarce corporate resources sometime find business people asking lawyers undertake work that they really should not do (such as review and edit a routine letter to a supplier). Once the lawyers are involved, business people have been known to say that they "ran it by legal" and use that to mitigate the responsibility for an unsuccessful business arrangement. A quick test is if the in-house lawyer asks the "why" question: how does the client request for services implicate a business strategy or goal with legal risk implications?

Assuming the matter is within the role of the legal department, the primary lawyer is assigned along with others in the department. At this stage, the legal team – in collaboration with the client and other stakeholders – should reach agreement on the goals, objectives and scope of the matter. Time constraints should be specified (e.g. close the deal by the end of the fiscal year; settle the case before there is a change in business unit management). The business and legal risks should be assessed along with the complexity of the matter.

At this point, in-house counsel determines appropriate resources with a "make vs buy" decision: should work be completed exclusively in-house, or should outside counsel be engaged? If outside counsel is appropriate, it is essential to identify their role and the nature of the legal department relationship: is it collaboration, management, or outsourcing? Is there a go-to firm, or is there a panel of options available if the matter is put out to bid? What fee structures are appropriate if financial agreements are not already in place? Consideration of these issues will lead to well-informed decision-making.

Planning

Planning does not just happen on its own. Effective lawyers start the planning process to ensure that the scope of the work is well defined. This is the baseline for managing client expectations and guiding the work of the legal team. Clients express dissatisfaction when there is a gap between their needs and the lawyer's perception of her role. Team members are frustrated when work is inefficient, duplicative or incomplete. A Statement of Work should be developed, with sign-off by the business client. The frequency of status checks, communication and metrics for monitoring the matter should be determined early on. If outside counsel is to be involved, the retention and pricing arrangements need to be established in the initial planning stage. Development of a baseline plan and honest discussion at this stage is key to avoiding misunderstandings and tension as the matter unfolds.

While there are often too many meetings, the kick-off meeting is indispensable. As the forum for collaborative planning, it sets the tone for sound stewardship of resources, accountability of team members, and goals of sound economics and delivery of value. Rapid action and deliberative planning can co-exist even though lawyers typically seek to act and adjust, rather than plan and execute.

Several LPM tools are useful at this stage to guide the discussion and confirm the scope of work. They include the project charter, the stakeholder analysis and the work plan. Now is the time to discuss allocation of roles and responsibilities. A useful tool is a LACI/RACI chart. All of these tools are discussed in more detail below. If outside counsel is involved, a budget should be formulated as the work plan is developed.

It is critical to document the assumptions associated with the phases of work since they will be revisited as the matter evolves. It is also helpful to create a timeline or Gantt chart to reflect time constraints and the expected duration of phases of the matter. They too will be changed as the matter evolves, but having the estimate helps frame everyone's expectations about when they will need to be available. The work plan, Gantt chart and the LACI chart are tools that communicate the sequencing of events that affect clients and members of the legal team. When used effectively, bottlenecks and fire drills are significantly reduced – even eliminated. The discipline of planning by using relevant tools helps overcome the chaos of "ready, aim, fire!", which so many lawyers and clients have experienced.

Execution

Execution is the meat of handling the matter. In addition to the substantive legal work and engagement of the business client, there is also the need to continuously check that the work on the matter is meeting expectations.

1. **Scope**. Is the work being handled so that the scope that was established at the outset is on track? What needs to be managed to resist changes that do not meet the client's definition of success? Should anything else be monitored?
2. **Scope creep**. Is the work expanding for the legal team? Scope creep occurs when lawyers are asked to play a role that the client or a third party was expected to perform, circumstances change (facts, people or the law), assumptions made at the outset are unfounded, or unanticipated events occur. Does outside counsel have more work to do than reflected in the statement of work or work plan? Are their legal fee expectations still appropriate?
3. **Resource management**. Is the legal team contributing an unexpected level of effort? Although one reason may be scope creep, there also may be turnover in members of the legal team or stakeholders who require education and transition time.
4. **Costs**. If third parties, such as outside counsel, e-discovery vendors or contract lawyers are involved, how do fees and expenses compare to the budget? Variances need to be understood in detail, rather than characterized as overruns or poor budgeting. The timetable may have shifted with costs occurring earlier or later than expected.

Assumptions and the occurrence of "unknown unknowns" should be evaluated in reviewing a budget, forecast, and invoice.

5. **Outcomes**. Are the results meeting business and legal objectives for the matter as it evolves? The definition of success may change, so it is important to determine if the plan still meets current goals. For example, an M&A deal that was strategic when launched because the company was entering a new market may be a bolt-on acquisition because another deal closed earlier; a litigation that is critical to a core business may be less significant because the business has been sold. The law governing the matter may have changed. The level of risk and effort varies based on the business and legal context, which needs to be confirmed with the client throughout the matter.

A well-managed matter is not a series of ad-hoc reviews and scrambles to submit reports to management. It is an ongoing process that is embedded in regular and appropriate communication.

Review

Review is a stage that is often scuttled. It is all too easy to move on to the next matter and avoid any perception of failure. Nevertheless, the review stage is an excellent opportunity for legal teams to demonstrate the value of the legal department and their commitment to continuous improvement. In this stage, the client, in-house lead and outside counsel should evaluate the results, particularly how the matter was planned, managed and executed. Insights gathered during this stage ultimately lead to more successful outcomes and more efficient handling of similar work in the future.

During this stage, it is important to look for what worked well and should be replicated as a best practice. "Good work" should enhance future work – by engendering improved action plans, training opportunities and templates. Watch the tendency to be hypercritical; find the positive. Remember that common practice is not the same as "best practice". Strive to raise the bar.

Identify the source of any tension that emerged among team members or with the internal client. Fertile areas for review are moments when things seemed to go off track, when progress was marred by misunderstandings, duplicative work, and surprises. Focus on the root cause of variances from plan and the steps taken to recover. Shifting stakeholders may have materially changed the scope of work and strategy. Concerns about business reputation or relationships with suppliers and customers may have caused a dramatic change in plans. Matters that at one point were mission-critical may have diminished in importance.

The review stage is the opportunity to determine what factors fostered or detracted from efficiency and the client's view of value. Soliciting the client's feedback demonstrates the legal team's commitment to achieving client satisfaction and following best practices. At this stage, it is important to identify the root cause of problems which led to legal department involvement. This not only prevents legal problems from arising in the future; it also opens the door for the legal team to be proactive with its client. Lawyers also can take away a deeper understanding of the business; they increase their sophistication in identifying opportunities for clients derived from legal expertise. Finally, the learnings from the review stage reinforces the law department's understanding of how to most diplomatically manage the inappropriate demand of clients for law department participation.

Metrics

No discussion on LPM is complete without a discussion on how to measure its impact. In the business case and action plan[8] for LPM developed by a CLOC working group in 2017, the following chart in Figure 2shows where relevant metrics can be developed:

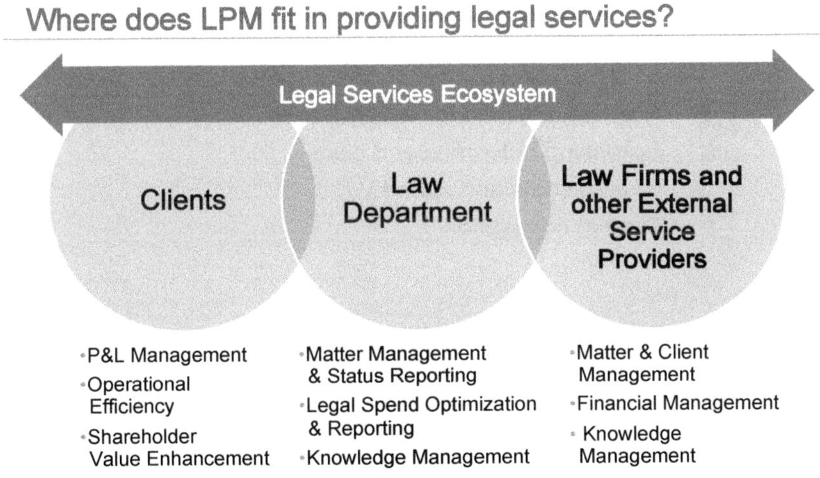

Figure 2: LPM business case and action plan. Source: https://cloc.org/industry-guidelines – CLOC Legal Project Management (LPM) for Legal Teams; The Business Case and Action Plan for Legal Departments

Clients and the general counsel focus on managing the bottom line and enhancing shareholder value. The corporate profit and loss statement is affected by the cost of legal services, measured by aggregating the compensation and benefits of members of the legal department, allocated corporate overhead, spending on outside counsel and other third parties, and out of pocket expenses. Shareholder value is enhanced by transactions and resolution of litigation that affect the corporate balance sheet. Matter management, legal spend optimization and knowledge management are derivatives of these corporate goals.

The well-managed legal department keeps its eyes on metrics that indicate the extent to which these practices are achieved. The law firm, when involved, addresses its own economic goals.

A legal department seeking to develop metrics should consider the results of LPM and which aspects are worth measuring, as highlighted in Figure 3.

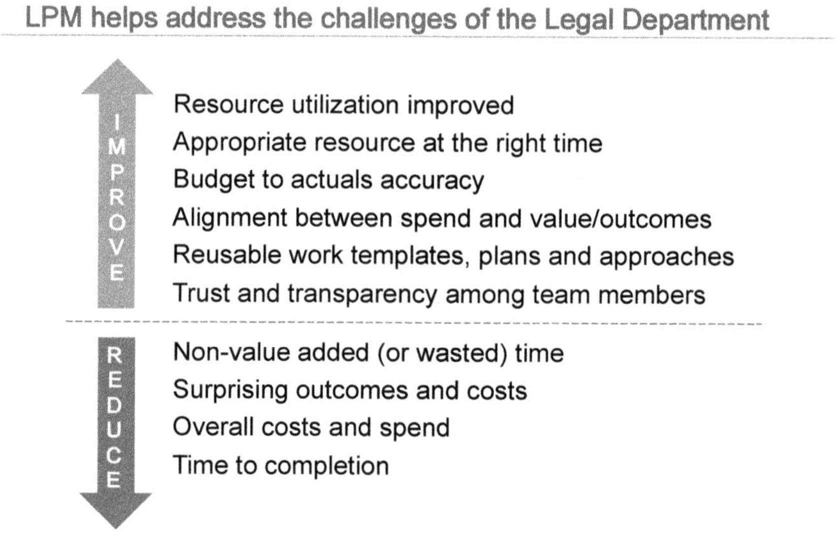

Figure 3: The results of LPM. Source: https://cloc.org/industry-guidelines - CLOC Legal Project Management (LPM) for Legal Teams; The Business Case and Action Plan for Legal Departments.

Conclusion

The role of lawyers in the corporate setting is to respond to a client's need for legal support in maximizing shareholder value and supporting corporate stewardship. Often the lawyer must guide the client to articulate the full range of business objectives and stakeholders in a situation. She evolves from the role of technical specialist and risk manager to a key participant in addressing business challenges and opportunities.

In-house counsel is uniquely situated to meld legal strategy and tactics with operational constraints that the business imposes. For most companies, this necessitates disciplined management of costs as well as the protection of its assets. Concurrently, counsel must model the behaviors that the client expects of other members of the business team: stewarding the client's resources and demonstrating accountability not only for what is done, but also for how it is done. In-house counsel manages the delivery of legal services to the client by focusing on a cost-effective action plan that achieves the client's business goals using the tools of legal project management.

The timely delivery of information is the life-blood of a legal matter; a formal communication plan is its circulatory system. At its core, LPM is about effective communication, which enables the legal team to demonstrate its value – and serve as a steward of corporate resources.

References

1. This chapter reflects many years of collaboration with the author's former colleagues at QLex Consulting Inc., James Buckley and Nancy Lasersohn. Jim is the pioneer of legal project management through his work as Associate General Counsel, Environmental Health and Safety at LockheedMartin Corporation as described in this three-part series 'Welcome to Lawyerland' in the ACC Docket (January–March 2005). After leaving Lockheed, he joined Nancy and me at QLex, where we introduced LPM to the DuPont Legal Department in 2011 under Thomas Sager's leadership as General Counsel and implementation support of Lynn Simpson, now at Chemours as a business process owner, Legal Operations. Tom has continued as an LPM proponent as a partner at Ballard Spahr LLP.
2. The chapter heavily references a working group that has developed a LPM business case and resource for Corporate Legal Operations Consortium (CLOC) under the leadership of Connie Brenton, Patrick Ellis and Pratik Patel. Special thanks go to Janelle Belling (Perkins Coie LLP), Kevin Bielawski (Husch Blackwell LLP), Danny Kotlowitz (Telstra), Patrick Ellis (GM), Dan Safran (Legal Shift) and David Rueff, Jr. (Baker Donelson) for their particular insights. https://www.law360.com/articles/537101, Law Practice is Evolving Via 'Legal Project Management' (May 15, 2014); wwww.aileenleventon.com/publications.
3. There are many frameworks, and they all support the same goal of managing the scope of work, planning and monitoring, and communication. Two examples that were developed for law firms are highlighted in S. Lambreth, A. Leventon and

D. Rueff, *Implementing Legal Project Management* (Createspace 2016). This book contains a detailed description of all the tools discussed in this chapter.

4. See https://cloc.org/industry-guidelines and to CLOC Legal Project Management (LPM) for Legal Teams. See also aileenleventon.com/services.
5. https://www.acc.com/legalresources/quickcounsel/lpm.cfm.
6. See http://www.edge.ai/2017/04/one-meeting-you-must-have/.
7. See Kleinman and Leventon, Better-Faster-Cheaper Through Legal Project Management: The LACI Chart, BNA Bloomberg, 2016.
8. See Note 4, above.

www.ingramcontent.com/pod-product-compliance
Ingram Content Group UK Ltd.
Pitfield, Milton Keynes, MK11 3LW, UK
UKHW021834131026
9310IPUK00004B/76

9 781783 583522